# The Little Guy Successfully Sued My Government!

# I have harassed his son and daughter ever since!

## Kerry Lynne Findlay

*This book is based on Former Classification Officer Terry Mallenby's recollections, supplemented by Personal Federal Court documents.*


*Terry Mallenby, BA, BSW, MA*
*Former Classification Officer*
*B.C. Maximum Security Penitentiary*
*Canadian Penitentiary Service*
*New Westminster, Canada*

**Index**                                        **Page**

**Chapter 1**

**Let's look at the players who harassed the "little guy" for successfully suing the government, one comes from British Columbia.**

That person is Kerry Lynne Findlay, Canada's Internal Revenue Minister:

Kerry Lynne D. Findlay Q.C.
#202 - 5000 Bridge Street
Delta, British Columbia V4K 2K4
Tel: 604 940 8040
Fax: 604 940-8041
Email: Kerry-Lynne.Findlay@parl.gc.ca

How pure is British Columbia or are they used to corruption?

As cited in "Stupidification of British Columbia / The BC Rail Corruption Scandal Stall Game":

*Classic baiting and switching performed like a Russian ballet, spins twirls and tosses, a stage busy with dancers, design and artists adorned in tutus and tight pants, eyes easily strained following all the moving parts, I don`t know if we should turn the BC Rail Saga into a ballet or tragic Shakespearian play, although the thought of Gordon Campbell and David Mclean prancing in tight pants is less than appetizing.*

Who were these pirouetting British Columbia "con artists"?

Gordon Campbell - Premier of British Columbia!

And, born in Calgary, David McLean grew up in Edmonton where his father was a train dispatcher with CN. He moved to Vancouver in 1968 and started the McLean Group in 1972!

Where does Gordon Campbell - Premier of British Columbia fit into the picture?

Oh, yes:

*The two men at the center of BC Rail corruption case — Dave Basi and Bob Virk — pleaded guilty Monday just as their trial was about to resume in B.C. Supreme Court in Vancouver.*

*In a statement read in court, the two former ministerial aides in Premier Gordon Campbell's Liberal government changed their pleas on four charges.*

*The two admitted providing insider information to interested parties in the 2003 sale of BC Rail and receiving benefits for the information, including money and ...*[1]

And, where does David McLean fit into the picture?

Ah, yes:

David McLean was one of Gordon Campbell's biggest and most long-standing supporters. [2]

David McLean was also the chair of CN Rail?

And guess what "CN Rail was one of the BC Liberal Party's most significant donors, contributing $113,000 between 1994 and 2004, and another $155,000 between 2005 and 2009."[3]

And guess what, "Court proceedings included evidence that Kinsella was paid $297,000 to advise BC Rail between 2002 and 2005. The railway's operations were sold to CN, headed by prominent BC Liberal donor David McLean, in late 2003."[4]

Followed by, "British Columbia is booming. At least it is if you're David McLean. Of all the British Columbians who've prospered under the Liberals' New Era, McLean might be the top of the list."[5]

Not enough British Columbia corruption yet?

Did the Canadian mainstream media help cover-up British Columbia corruption!

As reported:

*Premier Christy Clark Terminates Hyndman, Chairman of B.C. Securities Commission*

*Unreported in Canada's mainstream media and, to our knowledge first reported here, Premier Christy Clark, and her colleagues, fired or terminated Douglas Hyndman from his lofty sinecure as Chairman of the British Columbia Securities Commission by Order In Council made May 28, 2012. Mr. Hyndam was paid an obscene and outrageous salary (from British Columbia taxpayers money) of $523,000.00 in 2010/2011.*

*From 1987 to 2012, Douglas Hyndman was the man in responsible for supervising much of the activity at the Vancovuer Stock Exchange, one of the great crime scenes of the Western World.*

*At this time, we do not have enough information to determine if Douglas Hyndman is a crook but the investigation continues. Three weeks after he was terminated from the his top job, the story remains unreported by the mainstream media in Canada.*[6]

Even the British Columbia Attorney General Wally Oppal is apparently corrupt, according to this article "The Missing Women Fiasco. British Columbia Corruption", Posted on Thursday, February 23 at 19:52 by Robin Mathews

*The stories today spread out and take in the apparently well-meaning and apparently seriously pursued "Inquiry" into the Missing (murdered) Women of Vancouver's Downtown East End. The multiple murders were overlooked for years and years by the RCMP and the Vancouver police.*

*I say the "apparently well-meaning" Inquiry because I don't – for a tenth of a second - believe the Inquiry is well-meaning. I believe it is a huge whitewash and snow-job, a huge public relations boondoggle ... costing British Columbians millions of dollars.*

*Begin at the beginning. The Commissioner of the Inquiry is Wally Oppal. Wally Oppal was a Supreme Court judge and an Appeals Court judge in British Columbia. He did a large Inquiry into policing in British Columbia. He jumped from the court into the Liberal Party of Gordon Campbell and became the Attorney General of the Province. Obviously he was one of the best informed law officers in the Province.*

*As Attorney General he spent much time – in my judgement -preventing the legislature from having reasonable information through answers to questions asked in session and in the foyers of the legislature– about the B.C. Rail Scandal and the connected criminal case against government aides Dave Basi, Bobby Virk, and Aneal Basi. In my opinion Oppal disgraced the position of Attorney General, made it a clown's role and a ridiculously partisan charade. In my opinion he refused to answer perfectly acceptable questions – which he had an obligation to answer as Attorney General.*

*But he got caught. And so we can move beyond political analysis and my opinion to fact ... undoubted fact.*

*Wanting to make a case against the alleged bigamists in the Bountiful settlement in B.C., Oppal set to work to have a case taken against them. [I*

*happen to believe he did so to garner approval for the Campbell government, deteriorating in public regard. Playing a political game with justice.]*

*The process for taking such a case is for the Attorney General to go to a distinguished private lawyer and to place the matter in his/her hands. In that way, government is saying "we think there is grounds here for action, but to make sure it is not seen as a political move, we place it in the hands of reputable counsel who will make the decision to proceed or not to proceed – ON THE BASIS OF LAW. The Special Prosecutor we appoint will make the decision."*

*Wally Oppal went to lawyer (Special Prosecutor) number one. The lawyer said don't take a case. First Canada has to know if the Charter of Rights and Freedoms says that bigamy - as an expression of Religious Faith - is acceptable. No case can be fought until that matter has been decided. So Wally Oppal went to another lawyer. Wally Oppal wanted a case. The second lawyer said exactly what the first lawyer said: don't take a case until Canada knows what the Charter of Rights and Freedoms says about bigamy as an expression of Religious Faith.*

*And so Wally Oppal went to another lawyer appointed as Special Prosecutor. And – third time good luck for Oppal! That lawyer said that he'd take a case, now, against the Bountiful bigamists. Wally Oppal wanted action, we may believe, for political reasons - not for reasons of the administration of justice.*

*The case against the bigamists of Bountiful began in B.C. Supreme Court. Counsel for the Defence pointed out to the judge that Wally Oppal, Attorney General of the Province, the highest law officer of the Crown, had refused the decision of two appointed Special Prosecutors, had gone around them to a third, until he had a case before her.*

*The judge on the case didn't waste any time. She referred to Wally Oppal's Special Prosecutor shopping – to what was, in fact, the misuse of the whole process. And she threw the case out of court right then and there. Done.[7]*

No wonder the British Columbia Mounted Police can get away with murder, Wally Oppal is the British Columbia Attorney General [see Appendices below]?[8]

**Footnotes**

1. BC Rail corruption trial ends with guilty pleas
CBC News, Posted: Oct 18, 2010

2 - 3. How BC Rail Was Made to Disappear
By Bill Tieleman, 27 Dec 2011, TheTyee.ca

4. BC Liberal Ultra-Insider Kinsella Switching to Arizona?
By Bob Mackin, 28 Mar 2013, TheTyee.ca

5. How Gordon Campbell's Policies Made a Rich Friend Far Richer:
Longtime Campbell ally David McLean chairs CN Rail and owns a film
studio. BC Liberal decisions helped those firms reap hundreds of millions
of dollars.  By Richard Warnica, 9 May 2005, TheTyee.ca

6. Corruption Clean Up Continuing in British Columbia
 Water War Crimes, June 20, 2010

7. The Missing Women Fiasco. British Columbia Corruption
Posted on Thursday, February 23 at 19:52 by Robin Mathews

8. Still they get no consequences.
By Suzanne Fournier, The Province.

**Chapter 2**

**What are the federal police like in British Columbia?**

Apparently no better!

As cited in 'Still they get no consequences', four Mounties involved should not get off scot-free, says Dziekanski's mother, reported by Suzanne Fournier, The Province June 20, 2010.

Zofia Cisowski's "darkest hour" after learning that her son Robert Dziekanski was dead came when B.C. criminal justice officials declared that the RCMP had done nothing wrong -- and that it was her son's own fault that he died.

Now that she has been vindicated by the Braidwood Inquiry report castigating the officers and ruling her son did nothing wrong, Cisowski still carries with her a news clipping containing the earlier blaming, hurtful words.

On Dec. 12, 2008, B.C. Criminal Justice branch spokesman Stan Lowe "cleared" the four officers of any wrongdoing and portrayed Dziekanski as a violent and agitated alcoholic whose irrational behaviour contributed to his own death.

Last week, Walter Kosteckyj, Cisowski's lawyer, said "that was Zofia's darkest hour, after losing her son, and that's why she still carries that news clipping with her."

So far, Cisowski notes, none of the four Mounties "has ever got any consequences."

On Friday, Cisowski had the satisfaction of hearing Thomas Braidwood call the four Mounties "inappropriately aggressive" and "patently unbelievable," while emphasizing Dziekanski did nothing wrong nor in any way caused his own death.

"This tragic case is at its heart the story of shameful conduct by a few officers," Braidwood said.

"It ought not to reflect unfairly on the many thousands of RCMP and other police officers who have protected our communities and earned a well-deserved reputation in doing so."

Cisowski heard B.C. Attorney-General Mike de Jong promise to appoint a special prosecutor and commit to a citizen-led Independent Investigation

Office to conduct criminal investigations into RCMP or municipal police incidents causing death or harm.

Friday was an exhausting day after a night in which Cisowski slept little, coming at the end of years of hearings in which a video of her son's death was screened repeatedly -- although it helped a kind and patient former judge get to the truth.

Braidwood called the bystandervideo by Paul Pritchard of Dziekanski's Tasering death "invaluable" evidence that "couldn't be cross-examined."

Cisowski received an apology Friday from the RCMP's top cop, Commissioner William Elliott.

Yet as a mother, Cisowski did not hear from Elliott -- the first lawyer and non-cop to head the national RCMP -- the words she has waited so long to hear, she said.

"Nothing will happen to them, still they are on the job, the four policemen who caused Robert's death by what they did, and then they lie," said Cisowski.

Listening to Elliott say the RCMP has reformed its training and Taser policies, Cisowski whispered: "Still they get no consequences for causing my son's death."

Braidwood's 460-page report, entitled simply Why? The Robert Dziekanski Tragedy, is a blistering denunciation of the four Mounties who Tasered and restrained Dziekanski face down, then left him unattended until he died.

Onlookers were incredulous when Elliott said Friday he wouldn't be announcing any disciplinary measures for any of the four Mounties for their role in Dziekanski's death. He said he would await the special prosecutor's report.

Elliott acknowledged that Cpl. Benjamin Monty Robinson is suspended with pay, but only in connection with the unrelated traffic death of a motorcyclist. That matter doesn't go to trial until April 2011.

The other three -- Const. Gerry Rundel, Const. Bill Bentley and Const. Kwesi Millington -- are "on the job but not in front-line policing," said Elliott, who couldn't explain why the four officers could be criticized about an unjustified death and yet remain on the RCMP payroll.

Elliott hinted it might even be too late to mete out internal punishment, but admitted: "We recognize there needs to be fairly fundamental changes in our discipline system."

Braidwood said the four Mounties behaved as if they were responding to a "barroom brawl," and senior officer Robinson "intervened in an inappropriately aggressive manner."

"I found that Mr. Dziekanski had been compliant, was not defiant or resistant, did not brandish the stapler and did not move toward any of the officers," Braidwood said.

"I concluded the constable [Millington] was not justified in deploying the weapon and neither the constable nor the corporal honestly perceived that Mr. Dziekanski was intending to attack any of the officers."

Braidwood said the other two officers also "offered patently unbelievable after-the-fact rationalizations of their police notes and statements to [the Integrated Homicide Investigation Team]."

As for Robinson's claim that the Mounties made a point to check if Dziekanski was alive, Braidwood was dismissive.

"I can place little reliance on the testimony of Cpl. Robinson that he constantly monitored Mr. Dziekanski's breathing until the firefighters arrived. Similarly, I find unpersuasive the testimony of Const. Rundel that . . . he knelt down near Mr. Dziekanski and heard him breathing and snoring.

"I am satisfied that Mr. Dziekanski went into cardiac arrest first, then went unconscious, and finally showed signs of cyanosis, all within 75 seconds of being handcuffed."

De Jong was prompt to appoint special prosecutor Richard Peck to look into possible criminal charges against the four Mounties.

"There was misconduct here and that reflects badly [on the RCMP]," said de Jong.

"The human dimension in this is staggering, that someone would be lost within an airport for hours, separated by a glass door forever from one of his loved ones."

The stark images on the Pritchard film, of the police behaviour and a man's death, had enormous impact, said De Jong.

"Many people [not just in B.C.] remember where they were at the time the film was shown," he said.

"We are welcoming and one of the friendliest countries in the world -- we didn't display it that day."

**Chapter 3**

**"No one but a moron overlooks the import of an e-mail like this"!**

The case involving the vicious tasering to death of 40-year-old Polish immigrant Robert Dziekanski warrants an additional chapter to see the extent of the lies by the Federal police in British Columbia.

As noted, "we have seen often-quoted Mountie mouthpiece Cpl. Dale Carr tell the Braidwood inquiry that top RCMP brass made a deliberate decision not to correct misinformation RCMP had given to the media about Dziekanski's death."[1]

In fact, "e-mail suggests four RCMP Officers committed perjury while senior officers sat silent,"[2] specifically suggests Mounties planned to deploy Taser before they arrived at YVR, contrary to their testimony.[3]

As reported, "after months of outrage about the conduct of the four Mounties who responded to Vancouver Airport Oct. 14, 2007, who can believe that at the last minute, a federal lawyer would produce what many would consider a smoking gun -- an e-mail saying the officers decided to use the Taser before confronting the Polish immigrant?"[4]

"If true, the Nov. 5, 2007, e-mail titled "Media strategy -- release of the YVR video," from RCMP Chief Supt. Dick Bent to assistant commissioner Al McIntyre, establishes the four have been lying through their teeth. This critical document suggests the four officers committed perjury and that senior officers sat silent while they did so."[5]

"The documents that have just come to our attention include a critical e-mail from very high up in the RCMP chain of command, disclosing that the officers decided in a premeditated way, en route to the scene."[6]

Even the RCMP lawyers apparently lie?

"Lawyer Helen Roberts, who represents the RCMP at the inquiry, offered a tearful apology to inquiry commissioner Thomas Braidwood, a retired judge, for not disclosing the e-mail sooner."[7]

"Helen Roberts had every reason to be in tears Friday as she apologized to the public inquiry into Dziekanski's death for failing to disclose what appears to be not just germane but also startlingly important evidence."[8]

Robert's crocodile tears don't wash!

"If Roberts had cried over Dziekanski mother's pain, I would be moved --

but a veteran lawyer wet-eyed over another screw-up in this case? I think they were crocodile tears."[9]

"I find this delay in disclosing it to the commission appalling," Braidwood said. "The contents of this e-mail goes to the heart of this inquiry's work."[10]

"It should have been disclosed much, much sooner ... months and months ago."[11]

"It's a stunning turn of events," Don Rosenbloom, the lawyer representing the government of Poland at the inquiry.[12]

Rosenbloom said the 11th-hour disclosure "is totally inconsistent with testimony given under oath" and goes to the heart of the issue of police fabrication. During the hearing, he said, "we were alleging [the four Mounties] were fabricating their story."[13]

The RCMP fabrication was, in fact, true!

Dziekanski's mother told reporters she was surprised and angry about the e-mail being released so late. She suggested there had been a "coverup."[14]

"This is the kind of evidence someone should have known would have important consequences," said Walter Kosteckyj, the lawyer representing Dziekanski's mother at the inquiry.[15]

He said he had spent the last two weeks preparing his final arguments for the inquiry, only to find not all the evidence has been heard.[16]

The RCMP lawyer tries to white-wash the facts?

David Butcher, the lawyer representing Const. Bill Bentley, one of the four Mounties involved in the in-custody death, said Bent's e-mail was hearsay and not credible evidence.[17]

B.C. Attorney-General Mike de Jong said he was concerned about the new development, "the possibility that new evidence may be emerging at this late date is troubling, and I'm sure very troubling for the commission itself," he said.[18]

"Commissions of this sort, and really our system of justice, rely on all witnesses who give evidence under oath to provide truthful and honest answers."[19]

Incredibly, Commissioner William Elliott's carefully parsed press release was equally unbelievable: "This was simply an oversight. Unfortunately in an exercise of this magnitude, such an oversight can occur."[20]

Elliott a moron, as cited, "no one but a moron overlooks the import of an e-mail like this" [see Appendix 7a – 7c].[21]

That was not an "oversight." It was professional incompetence or a cover-up.[22]

Paul Kennedy, the chairman of the Commission for Public Complaints Against the RCMP, using a news conference in Vancouver, took some well-aimed verbal shots at stagnant RCMP culture, especially its notorious, self-destructive resistance to change. It is a "massively inert" organization, he said, and that must not stand.[23]

Footnotes

1. *RCMP admissions in Dziekanski Taser death are troubling.* By Damian Inwood, Wed, Apr 22 2009.

2. *E-mail Suggests Four RCMP Officers Committed Perjury While Senior Officers Sat Silent.* Contributed on Sun, 2009/06/21 - 2:30pm.

3. *Startling New Email Halts Inquiry.* By Neal Hall and Lori Culbert; June 20, 2009 - Vancouver Sun.

4 - 5. *Damning e-mail suggests the four officers committed perjury and that senior officers sat silent while they did.* By Ian Mulgrew; June 20, 2009 - Vancouver Sun.

6 - 7. *Startling New Email Halts Inquiry.* By Neal Hall and Lori Culbert; June 20, 2009 - Vancouver Sun.

8 - 9. *Damning e-mail suggests the four officers committed perjury and that senior officers sat silent while they did.* By Ian Mulgrew; June 20, 2009 - Vancouver Sun.

10 - 19. *Startling New Email Halts Inquiry.* By Neal Hall and Lori Culbert; June 20, 2009 - Vancouver Sun.

20 - 22. *Damning e-mail suggests the four officers committed perjury and that senior officers sat silent while they did.* By Ian Mulgrew; June 20, 2009 - Vancouver Sun.

23. *RCMP watchdog goes out firing with Dziekanski report.* Posted: December 08, 2009 by Ron Nurwisah, Brian Hutchinson, National Post.

## Chapter 4

**Damning e-mail suggests the four federal police officers committed perjury in British Columbia!**

As cited in "Mounties in Tasering should face prosecution: Damning e-mail suggests the four RCMP officers committed perjury and that senior RCMP officers sat silent while they did", by Ian Mulgrew; June 20, 2009 - Vancouver Sun.

The Braidwood Inquiry into the Taser-related death of Robert Dziekanski has been blown up and left in ruins by the revelation a key RCMP e-mail was withheld from the commission.

After months of outrage about the conduct of the four Mounties who responded to Vancouver Airport Oct. 14, 2007, who can believe that at the last minute, a federal lawyer would produce what many would consider a smoking gun -- an e-mail saying the officers decided to use the Taser before confronting the Polish immigrant?

If true, the Nov. 5, 2007, e-mail titled "Media strategy -- release of the YVR video," from RCMP Chief Supt. Dick Bent to assistant commissioner Al McIntyre, establishes the four have been lying through their teeth.

This critical document suggests the four officers committed perjury and that senior officers sat silent while they did so. Worse, it seems there are many other documents that have not been turned over that may be relevant.

This e-mail was one of 260 documents on a CD sent by the RCMP to the justice department last April, yet the federal lawyers didn't open the CD until last week.

Last week? Evidence delivered in April didn't get opened until last week?

What?

Helen Roberts had every reason to be in tears Friday as she apologized to the public inquiry into Dziekanski's death for failing to disclose what appears to be not just germane but also startlingly important evidence.

If Roberts had cried over Dziekanski mother's pain, I would be moved -- but a veteran lawyer wet-eyed over another screw-up in this case? I think they were crocodile tears.

Commissioner William Elliott's carefully parsed press release was equally unbelievable: "This was simply an oversight. Unfortunately in an exercise of this magnitude, such an oversight can occur."

Bollocks. No one but a moron overlooks the import of an e-mail like this.

The officers deny the explosive content is true and Roberts says Bent was wrong in what he said. But their protestations ring hollow after almost 18 months of bluster and denial. So does Elliott's threadbare these-things-happen excuse.

The situation is as bad as the most virulent critics of the Mounties feared. This is no longer about four officers who made mistakes in judgment: It's about an organization that thinks it is above the law.

"I find this delay in disclosing it to the commission appalling," an upset Braidwood said. "The contents of this e-mail goes to the heart of this inquiry's work."

Exactly.

Braidwood says his inquiry will resume on Sept. 22 after commission lawyers have time to review the e-mail, conduct an investigation and perhaps call the senior Mounties to testify about the document.

I think not.

There was a time when I thought Oct. 14, 2007 was the day that would live in the annals of RCMP infamy, but June 19, 2009 has eclipsed the tragedy of Dziekanski's death.

On Friday, a country's faith in a once proud, once revered institution died.

We have left the realm of how to regulate Taser use and the circumstances of Dziekanski's death and entered the world of criminal conduct -- which is beyond Braidwood's provincially rooted authority to investigate.

If we needed any prod to reopen the decision not to prosecute these officers, we now have been given it.

It is time to thank commissioner Braidwood for his excellent work in bringing these unsettling facts to light and it's time to appoint a special prosecutor.

The B.C. Law Society should also begin an investigation into the conduct of Roberts and any other federal lawyer involved in this staggering lack of disclosure.

That was not an "oversight." It was professional incompetence or a cover-up.

## Chapter 5

**E-mail suggests four federal police committed perjury in British Columbia!**

As cited in "E-mail Suggests Four RCMP Officers Committed Perjury While Senior Officers Sat Silent" by Neal Hall and Lori Culbert; June 20, 2009 - Vancouver Sun.

Startling New Email Halts Inquiry, suggests Mounties planned to deploy Taser before they arrived at YVR, contrary to their testimony.

A shocking e-mail found last week brought the Braidwood inquiry to a sudden halt Friday and may result in the most senior RCMP officers in B.C. being required to testify.

The e-mail, sent by RCMP Chief Supt. Dick Bent to Assistant Commissioner Al Macintyre suggested for the first time that the four Mounties who responded to a call at Vancouver's airport planned to use a Taser on Robert Dziekanski, who died at the airport on Oct. 14, 2007, after he was Tasered five times.

Under the subject line "Media Strategy - Release of YVR video," the e-mail, dated Nov. 5, 2007, said: "Finally spoke to [Supt.] Wayne [Rideout] and he indicated that the members did not articulate that they saw the symptoms of excited delirium, but instead had discussed the response en route and decided that if he did not comply that they would go to CEW [conducted energy weapon]."

Lawyers for the four RCMP officers involved in the fatal incident said Friday their clients deny they formulated a plan to use a Taser on Dziekanski.

The officers testified at the inquiry they arrived in separate police cars and had no discussion beforehand.

Alex Pringle, a lawyer representing Rideout, who was in charge of investigating Dziekanski's death, appeared at the inquiry Friday and read a statement from his client, which said Bent's e-mail was in error. Pringle said it was a "misunderstanding of a conversation I had with him."

Lawyer Helen Roberts, who represents the RCMP at the inquiry, offered a tearful apology to inquiry commissioner Thomas Braidwood, a retired judge, for not disclosing the e-mail sooner.

She also said Bent was mistaken in his e-mail and that the officers did not plan to use the Taser. She offered to have senior Mounties testify.

"I find this delay in disclosing it to the commission appalling," Braidwood said. "The contents of this e-mail goes to the heart of this inquiry's work."

The e-mail will have to be investigated and further hearings may be required, the commissioner said.

He ordered the inquiry adjourned until Sept. 22. The delay was due to summer plans already made by many of the lawyers involved in the inquiry, he added.

Friday was supposed to be the start of final submissions by lawyers representing various parties, including the four Mounties involved in the in-custody death.

Commission counsel Art Vertlieb told the inquiry that the new e-mail was disclosed Tuesday by lawyers for the federal justice department, which represents the RCMP.

"It should have been disclosed much, much sooner ... months and months ago," Vertlieb later told reporters, adding he was "upset and frustrated" by the last-minute disclosure.

He said he didn't know whether the RCMP disclosed the e-mail to Crown counsel before a decision was made that no criminal charges were warranted against the four officers.

Vertlieb told the inquiry that the Bent e-mail was among 260 documents on a CD sent by the RCMP to the justice department in April, just before RCMP media relations officers testified at the inquiry about the botched handling of information released to the media in the days after Dziekanski's death.

He said the federal lawyers didn't open the CD until last week, discovering the Bent e-mail and other documents.

"It's a stunning turn of events," Don Rosenbloom, the lawyer representing the government of Poland at the inquiry, told reporters after the commissioner ordered the three-month adjournment.

"The documents that have just come to our attention include a critical e-mail from very high up in the RCMP chain of command, disclosing that the officers decided in a premeditated way, en route to the scene, to use the Taser if Mr. Dziekanski did not comply."

Rosenbloom said the 11th-hour disclosure "is totally inconsistent with testimony given under oath" and goes to the heart of the issue of police fabrication.

During the hearing, he said, "we were alleging [the four Mounties] were fabricating their story."

Dziekanski's mother told reporters she was surprised and angry about the e-mail being released so late. She suggested there had been a "coverup."

"This is the kind of evidence someone should have known would have important consequences," said Walter Kosteckyj, the lawyer representing Dziekanski's mother at the inquiry.

He said he had spent the last two weeks preparing his final arguments for the inquiry, only to find not all the evidence has been heard.

David Butcher, the lawyer representing Const. Bill Bentley, one of the four Mounties involved in the in-custody death, said Bent's e-mail was hearsay and not credible evidence.

"The chief superintendent is simply wrong," he said.

The late disclosure of the e-mail was the result of an oversight, RCMP Commissioner William Elliott said in a statement issued Friday.

"We have produced thousands of documents to our legal counsel for their review and for them to transmit all relevant material to the commission," Elliott said, pointing out that it was the RCMP that brought the Bent e-mail to the attention of the inquiry commissioner on Friday.

"Commissioner Braidwood was informed that a specific document was not provided and he himself accepted the government of Canada's sincere apologies for this oversight," Elliott's statement said.

"The RCMP wants all of the facts surrounding this tragic event to be known so that we can learn as much as possible and make any further required changes to the RCMP's policies and practices."

B.C. Attorney-General Mike de Jong said he was concerned about the new development.

"The possibility that new evidence may be emerging at this late date is troubling, and I'm sure very troubling for the commission itself," he said.

"Commissions of this sort, and really our system of justice, rely on all witnesses who give evidence under oath to provide truthful and honest answers."

Whether the testimony in the Dziekanski inquiry has been truthful will be up to Braidwood to decide, de Jong said. It will be up to Braidwood to assess the new evidence and determine its relevance before making his findings, he said, adding that it was too early to comment on the possible fallout from Friday's events.

The attorney-general said it would be premature to comment on whether criminal charges against the four officers should be reconsidered.

"I'm not going to rule anything in or out. I am going to wait with keen interest for Mr. Braidwood's report."

Dziekanski, who spoke no English, had travelled for 24 hours from Poland and spent about 10 hours at the airport, unable to find his mother, who went home to Kamloops after being told by officials that her son couldn't be found.

The 40-year-old man eventually started throwing around furniture, prompting a bystander to call 911.

Seconds after four Mounties arrived, Dziekanski was Tasered. He died at the scene.

**Chapter 6**

**The federal police had decided to electrocute him before they even saw him.**

As cited in "They had decided to electrocute him before they even saw him" by Rusty Idols, New Democrats Online.

In the car on the way to the airport as revealed in an email the government finally revealed on what was supposed to be the last day of the Braidwood Commission.

And you thought the RCMP's behavior couldn't look any worse.

This e-mail was one of 260 documents on a CD sent by the RCMP to the justice department last April, yet the federal lawyers didn't open the CD until last week.

Last week? Evidence delivered in April didn't get opened until last week?

What?

Helen Roberts had every reason to be in tears Friday as she apologized to the public inquiry into Dziekanski's death for failing to disclose what appears to be not just germane but also startlingly important evidence.

If Roberts had cried over Dziekanski mother's pain, I would be moved — but a veteran lawyer wet-eyed over another screw-up in this case? I think they were crocodile tears.

Commissioner William Elliott's carefully parsed press release was equally unbelievable: "This was simply an oversight. Unfortunately in an exercise of this magnitude, such an oversight can occur."

Bollocks. No one but a moron overlooks the import of an e-mail like this.

The officers deny the explosive content is true and Roberts says Bent was wrong in what he said. But their protestations ring hollow after almost 18 months of bluster and denial. So does Elliott's threadbare these-things-happen excuse.

The situation is as bad as the most virulent critics of the Mounties feared. This is no longer about four officers who made mistakes in judgment: It's about an organization that thinks it is above the law.

**Chapter 7**

**Let's look at the players, another comes from Newfoundland.**

Guess what, the same person from British Columbia is also in charge of the Newfoundland income tax center where the second person in this story comes from.

That person in charge of the Newfoundland income tax center is none other than Kerry Lynne Findlay, Canada's Internal Revenue Minister:

Kerry Lynne D. Findlay Q.C.
#202 - 5000 Bridge Street
Delta, British Columbia V4K 2K4
Tel: 604 940 8040
Fax: 604 940-8041
Email: Kerry-Lynne.Findlay@parl.gc.ca

You would think the Newfoundland government would have learned from the Mount Cashel scandal – a disgusting episode of child abuse to beat anything in past history?[1]

*"CAUTION": Before you go any further, I must tell you however that Newfoundland is not just a quaint tourist destination, as the following pretty little countryside and seascape photos might suggest ...*

*"Newfoundland is also infamous for its indifference to one of its most precious resources; its orphaned, unwanted foster children. Childhood sexual abuse has long been rampant and continues to receive justice's blind eye. ...*

*Not only sex abuse of children but an elitist attitude allowing misery upon misery to be heaped upon children of a physical and psychological nature by Newfoundland social workers ...[2]*

*Mount Cashel, a prominent institution that ran for more than a century in the east end of St. John's Newfoundland before a sexual abuse scandal erupted in 1989, triggering a harrowing public inquiry and a series of criminal convictions ...*

*The settlement is worth more than $16.5 million, which will be put into a trust ...*

*"This is not nearly enough money to fully satisfy 400 claims," said Geoff Budden, who represented about 90 clients, most of whom were residents of Mount Cashel ...*

*Lawyers in Newfoundland are pursuing litigation against parties that include the Newfoundland and Labrador government ...*

*The Mount Cashel Orphanage, which was the subject of the Hughes inquiry into the failure of the Newfoundland justice and Newfoundland social services systems ...*[3]

*St. John's, Newfoundland – A long-time resident of the Mount Cashel orphanage testified yesterday that former Christian Brother Stephen Rooney often fondled him and forced him to perform sex acts three times.*

*Rooney, a native of British Columbia, is the first of eight current or former Christian Brothers to go to trial on sex-related charges ...*[4]

Even a more recent episode was a Whistleblower that told Newfoundland Social Services Minister Kay Young and Newfoundland Premier Clyde Wells that their Youth Center, the Whibourne Center, had security problems!

Did Newfoundland Social Services Minister Kay Young and Newfoundland Premier Clyde Wells listen to him, no – they did not!

They didn't listen to the Whistleblower!

Instead they fabricated some cock-and-bull excuse and got rid of him!!

And what did Social Services Minister Kay Young do?

She even violated the violation of the Freedom of Information Act and the Privacy Act to make sure this PTSD sufferers name was revealed to the media [see below]?

What an unprofessional "cur"!

As cited, we can see that "mongrel's" comments here:

*November 16, 1994*
*HOUSE OF ASSEMBLY PROCEEDINGS*
*Vol. XLII No. 62*
http://www.assembly.nl.ca/business/hansard/ga42session2/94-11-16.htm

MR. FITZGERALD:

*Thank you, Mr. Speaker.*

*My question is to the Minister of Social Services. I want to ask the Minister of Social Services why she released information on the employment history of a Mr. xx, the former operations manager at the Newfoundland and Labrador Youth Center, in clear violation of the Freedom of Information Act and in violation I believe of the Privacy Act?*

MR. FITZGERALD:

*Mr. Speaker, not only did the minister violate the Freedom of Information and Privacy Act but she also gave false information, Mr. Speaker, about Mr. xx's employment history. The minister said that Mr. xx had been fired for reasons related to job performance.*

*The official record of employment the department gave to Mr. xx and to Employment Canada says he was dismissed for breach of trust and loss of confidence.*

*Now I ask the minister, did the minister know, Mr. Speaker, that she was giving false information in her press release?*

*Will she now admit Mr. xx was fired because he blew the whistle and disclosed the information as to what was actually happening out at the Newfoundland and Labrador Youth Center?*

Quite literally, this "mutt", Social Services Minister Kay Young revealed this PTSD sufferers name / Terry Mallenby's name to the media because he was trying to improve the security for the Newfoundland and Labrador Youth Center, the Whitbourne Center!

Now comes the next "sleaze-ball" Newfoundland Premier Clyde Wells:

*November 17, 1994*
*HOUSE OF ASSEMBLY PROCEEDINGS*
*Vol. XLII No. 63*
http://www.assembly.nl.ca/business/hansard/ga42session2/94-11-17.htm

MR. W. MATTHEWS:

*Thank you very much, Mr. Speaker.*

*I have a question for the Premier, following up on the line of questioning by the member for Bonavista South yesterday dealing with the Minister of Social Services Kay Young.*

*Now, on November 8, 1994 the Minister of Social Services Kay Young issued a public statement, a written press release, where she referred to the dismissal of one Mr. xx at the Newfoundland and Labrador Youth Center at Whitbourne.*

*In that she talked about the reasons for dismissal, job performance and work history.*

*I want to ask the Premier, in light of the minister's public statement that is clearly a violation of the Freedom of Information Act and the Privacy Act, but particularly the Freedom Information Act, section 10 (1) (b): Does the Premier consider this conduct and behavior of the Minister of Social Services Kay Young to be acceptable?*

MR. W. MATTHEWS:

*- and in that written, deliberate statement pertaining to the situation, she said: Mr. xx was dismissed for work related problems, job performance.*

*Now the record of employment belonging to Mr. xx states that he was dismissed for breach of trust and loss of confidence, so in essence, the minister in her statement, issued a false statement.*

*The reason was inaccurate and incorrect, so I want to ask the Premier: does he feel that the conduct of the Minister of Social Services Kay Young, in issuing a false, public statement is behaviour and conduct acceptable for a minister of his Administration or, is he going to allow the standards and behaviour and conduct of the ministers to sink to an all-time low in this Province, where, individual privacy will no longer be protected?*

Quite literally, this other "mutt", Newfoundland Premier Clyde Wells also revealed this PTSD sufferers name to the media simply because he was trying to improve the security for the Newfoundland and Labrador Youth Center, the Whitbourne Center!

The consequence:

What happened a year later, because these two "mutts" didn't listen to the "little guy"?

Due to the lax security, one of the youth committed suicide and a stink was raised about Newfoundland Premier Clyde Wells and Newfoundland Social Services Minister Kay Young ignoring this "little guy's"!

*1995 Death at Newfoundland Social Services Minister Kay Young's Whitbourne Youth Center*
October 8, 1999 (Justice)

*1999 Death at Newfoundland Social Services Minister Kay Young's*
*Whitbourne Youth Center*
News Release NLIS 4 March 1, 2001 (Justice)

*Attempted Suicide*
News Release, NLIS 5; May 29, 2000 (Justice)

*Another Attempted Suicide*
News Release, NLIS 2; June 29, 2000 (Justice)

*Parent concerned about son's treatment*
Published on Febuary 14th, 2008
Published on July 2nd, 2010
Barb Sweet, The Telegram

*Escape bid foiled at N.L. corrections facility.*
Last Updated: Saturday, December 11, 2010
CBC News

*N.L. young offenders assault, restrain staff in escape attempt*
Published On Sat Dec 11 2010

What a pair of "sleaze-balls"!

And why did these two "morons" do that, was it simply because the "little guy" had successfully sued Kerry Lynne Findlay's government?

Footnotes

1 - 2. Mount Cashel Orphanage ~ Institutionalized Pedophilia in St. John's Newfoundland

3. Mount Cashel abuse settlement sets stage for more suits

4. Christian Brother forced sex acts at Mount Cashel, ex-resident says

**The "little guy" was diagnosed with a multitude of disorders as a consequence of Kerry Lynne Findlay's federal police lies, illegal acts, harassment and other abuse.**

Author's note: Anyone who has to identify a loved-one in the morgue can appreciate the horror, grief, anger one experiences?

September 24th, 1996

The Medical Advisor
Income Security Programs
333 River Rd
Ottawa, Ontario
K1A 9Z9

OCT 7 1996

Dear Sir or Madame:

     Re:

     I am writing a letter on behalf of            one of my patients who suffers from a grievous mental malady. He has been previously accepted for CPP disability.

     His case is complicated. He is a very accomplished gentleman who has two advanced degrees including a Ph.D. and yet cannot work. He spends his time largely sequestered at home writing notes and letters and suffers extreme anxiety if he attempts to go outside.

     He is very secretive about events that happened in the past but evidently he sustained a major personal loss in 1976 and ever since then has never recovered. He has paranoid ideas and symptoms of marked anxiety. I have been treating him as best I could as a family physician but felt his symptoms were aggravated and complicated enough that I referred him to a psychiatrist.

               suffers from many symptoms of post-traumatic stress disorder and unresolved grief.....fear, guilt, horror, dreams of traumatic content, social avoidancy, decreased interest, impaired memory, irritability, anger, increased vigilance, sense of futility regarding the future, some paranoid ideations.

**Author's note: Anyone who has to identify a loved-one in the morgue can appreciate the horror, grief, anger one experiences?**

October 17, 1996


FRANCOISE LeBLANC, R.N., B.A.,
DISABILITY OPERATIONS DIVISION
333 RIVER ROAD
OTTAWA, CANADA    K1A 0L1

RE:
---------------------------------------------------------------------------------

Dear Francoise,

Thank you for your letter of October 1, 1996

gives a 20 year history of Post-Traumatic Stress Disorder following the homicide of a colleague in a prison uprising  and also the murder          in 1976. I believe you are well aware of these events and that           was falsely accused of the latter crime. The effect on his family relationships and on him are also well documented.           has become very suspicious of others especially Government agencies and is somewhat paranoid. This paranoia has made it difficult for him to accept psychological help as a degree of trust is almost essential. He seems to have made numerous attempts to improve his occupational situation, but his difficulties dealing with others always overwhelm him.

When seen,           exhibited and described numerous signs and symptoms of Post-Traumatic Stress Disorder including marked agitation whenever the subject of the murder loomed. He described fear, guilt and horror, traumatic dreams, social avoidance, loss of interest, poor memory for details of the murder, irritability, anger, increased vigilance, a sense of futility re. the future, difficulties with emotional involvement, and arousal by recollections of the trauma including those precipitated by news stories of similar events. In interviews, he is often tearful ,distraught and agitated.

Diagnostically, he has       1)      Post-Traumatic Stress Disorder -Chronic Type
                            2)      Social Phobia  -secondary to 1)

**Lifetime disability due to Kerry Lynne Findlay's federal police lies, illegal acts, and harassment!**

April 1, 1998

To: Mr. Denis Duhamel
Tower A, 11th floor
Place Vanier

From: Dr. N. Kanjilal
Medical Advisor

Subject:

As per your request, I reviewed the file of                    to determine the basis for granting him the disability benefits.

You are well aware that we are guided by the CPP Legislation which states that a person must be suffering from a physical and/or mental disability which is both severe and prolonged to be eligible to receive disability benefits. Severe means that the person must be incapable of pursuing any substantially gainful occupation regularly. Prolonged means that the incapacity to work at any substantially gainful occupation will likely be long continued and of indefinite duration. To assess such disability we have to ascertain the limiting loss or absence of the capacity to meet the occupational demands according to the regulatory requirements described above.

seems to have satisfied the legislation and in our judgement he is incapable to carry out any occupational demands.

will be well advised to consult his treating physicians if he wishes to find out about any particular medical condition, who will be in a better position to explain his specific question.

Hope this answers some of your problems. Please do not hesitate to contact me should you need any other information.

Dr. N. Kanjilal
Tel: 952-3620

33

**Chapter 8**

**Let's look at the previous Internal Revenue Minister Gail Shea who had harassed the "little guy" for successfully suing the government!**

What did this Internal Revenue Minister Gail Shea do?

Gail Shea knew full well that the little guy was on a fixed disability pension for PTSD!

However, for successfully suing the government, Gail Shea did bogus tax audits of him – as payback [see below]!

Is this why the current Internal Revenue Minister Kerry Lynne Findlay feels she can also harass the little guy's children for his successful suit of her government?

Kerry Lynne D. Findlay Q.C.
#202 - 5000 Bridge Street
Delta, British Columbia V4K 2K4
Tel: 604 940 8040
Fax: 604 940-8041
Email: Kerry-Lynne.Findlay@parl.gc.ca

There's always some "rat" with this government that will carry on the harassment!

**Bogus audit 2003 by Internal Revenue Minister Gail Shea!**

| Canada Revenue Agency | Agence du revenu du Canada | NOTICE OF REASSESSMENT | T491 E (10) |
|---|---|---|---|
| | | | 1 |

| Date | Name | Social insurance no. | Tax year | Tax centre |
|---|---|---|---|---|
| Jan 11, 2011 | WALLY MALLENBY | · · · · · | 2003 | |

0022050

At a later date, we may review your return to verify income you reported or deductions and credits you claimed. Keep all your slips, receipts, and other supporting documents in case we ask to see them.

Explanation of changes and other important information

This notice explains the results of our reassessment of your income tax return and any changes we may have made. Please refer to the "Summary" area for additional information.

We have adjusted your return to update your tuition and education amounts for carryforward.

We are mailing to you separately your reassessment notices for two or more taxation years. The notice for the latest taxation year will show your combined total refund or balance due. We will send you any refund to which you are entitled after we have reassessed all your returns.

According to this reassessment, you have unused federal and Ontario tuition and education amounts of $1,600 and $1,662, respectively, that you can carry forward to a future year.

If you have any questions about your reassessment, please call our Enquiries service at 1-800-959-8281. If you need to contact another area of the Agency, see the telephone listings in the government section of your telephone book.

**Bogus audit 2004 by Internal Revenue Minister Gail Shea!**

| Canada Revenue Agency | Agence du revenu du Canada | NOTICE OF REASSESSMENT | T491 E (10) |
|---|---|---|---|
| | | | 1 |

| Date | Name | Social insurance no. | Tax year | Tax centre |
|---|---|---|---|---|
| Jan 11, 2011 | WALLY MALLENBY | · · | 2004 | |

0022050

At a later date, we may review your return to verify income you reported or deductions and credits you claimed. Keep all your slips, receipts, and other supporting documents in case we ask to see them.

Explanation of changes and other important information

This notice explains the results of our reassessment of your income tax return and any changes we may have made. Please refer to the "Summary" area for additional information.

We have adjusted your return to update your tuition and education amounts for carryforward.

We are mailing to you separately your reassessment notices for two or more taxation years. The notice for the latest taxation year will show your combined total refund or balance due. We will send you any refund to which you are entitled after we have reassessed all your returns.

According to our records, you have unused federal and British Columbia tuition and education amounts of $1,600 and $1,600, respectively, that you can carry forward to a future year.

If you have any questions about your reassessment, please call our Enquiries service at 1-800-959-8281. If you need to contact another area of the Agency, see the telephone listings in the government section of your telephone book.

# Bogus audit 2005 by Internal Revenue Minister Gail Shea!

| ▌◆▌ Canada Revenue Agency | Agence du revenu du Canada | NOTICE OF REASSESSMENT | 7491 E (10) 1 |
|---|---|---|---|

| Date | Name | Social insurance no. | Tax year | Tax centre |
|---|---|---|---|---|
| Jan 11, 2011 | WALLY MALLENBY | | 2005 | |

DO22954

At a later date, we may review your return to verify income you reported or deductions and credits you claimed. Keep all your slips, receipts, and other supporting documents in case we ask to see them.

**Explanation of changes and other important information**

This notice explains the results of our reassessment of your income tax return and any changes we may have made. Please refer to the "Summary" area for additional information.

We have adjusted your return to update your tuition and education amounts for carryforward.

We are mailing to you separately your reassessment notices for two or more taxation years. The notice for the latest taxation year will show your combined total refund or balance due. We will send you any refund to which you are entitled after we have reassessed all your returns.

According to our records, you have unused federal and British Columbia tuition and education amounts of $1,600 and $1,600, respectively, that you can carry forward to a future year.

If you have any questions about your reassessment, please call our Enquiries service at 1-800-959-8281. If you need to contact another area of the Agency, see the telephone listings in the government section of your telephone book.

# Bogus audit 2006 by Internal Revenue Minister Gail Shea!

| ▌◆▌ Canada Revenue Agency | Agence du revenu du Canada | NOTICE OF REASSESSMENT | 7491 E (11) 1 |
|---|---|---|---|

| Date | Name | Social insurance no. | Tax year | Tax centre |
|---|---|---|---|---|
| Jan 11, 2011 | WALLY MALLENBY | | 2006 | |

DO22956

At a later date, we may review your return to verify income you reported or deductions and credits you claimed. Keep all your slips, receipts, and other supporting documents in case we ask to see them.

**Explanation of changes and other important information**

This notice explains the results of our reassessment of your income tax return and any changes we may have made. Please refer to the "Summary" area for additional information.

We have adjusted your return to update your tuition and education amounts for carryforward.

According to our records, you have unused federal tuition, education, and textbook amounts of $1,600 that you can carry forward to a future year.

According to our records, you have unused British Columbia tuition and education amounts of $1,600 that you can carry forward to a future year.

We are mailing to you separately your reassessment notices for two or more taxation years. The notice for the latest taxation year will show your combined total refund or balance due. We will send you any refund to which you are entitled after we have reassessed all your returns.

If you have any questions about your reassessment, please call our Enquiries service at 1-800-959-8281. If you need to contact another area of the Agency, see the telephone listings in the government section of your telephone book.

**Bogus audit 2007 by Internal Revenue Minister Gail Shea!**

Canada Revenue Agency — Agence du revenu du Canada

NOTICE OF REASSESSMENT

T491 E (10)

1

| Date | Name | Social insurance no. | Tax year | Tax centre |
|------|------|----------------------|----------|------------|
| Jan 11, 2011 | WALLY MALLENBY | | 2007 | |

0023088

At a later date, we may review your return to verify income you reported or deductions and credits you claimed. Keep all your slips, receipts, and other supporting documents in case we ask to see them.

Explanation of changes and other important information

This notice explains the results of our reassessment of your income tax return and any changes we may have made. Please refer to the "Summary" area for additional information.

We have adjusted your return to update your tuition and education amounts for carryforward.

According to our records, you have unused federal tuition, education, and textbook amounts of $1,600 that you can carry forward to a future year.

According to our records, you have unused British Columbia tuition and education amounts of $1,600 that you can carry forward to a future year.

We are mailing to you separately your reassessment notices for two or more taxation years. The notice for the latest taxation year will show your combined total refund or balance due. We will send you any refund to which you are entitled after we have reassessed all your returns.

If you have any questions about your reassessment, please call our Enquiries service at 1-800-959-8281. If you need to contact another area of the Agency, see the telephone listings in the government section of your telephone book.

**Bogus audit 2008 by Internal Revenue Minister Gail Shea!**

Canada Revenue Agency — Agence du revenu du Canada

NOTICE OF REASSESSMENT

T491 E (10)

1

| Date | Name | Social insurance no. | Tax year | Tax centre |
|------|------|----------------------|----------|------------|
| Jan 11, 2011 | WALLY MALLENBY | | 2008 | |

0072060

At a later date, we may review your return to verify income you reported or deductions and credits you claimed. Keep all your slips, receipts, and other supporting documents in case we ask to see them.

Explanation of changes and other important information

This notice explains the results of our reassessment of your income tax return and any changes we may have made. Please refer to the "Summary" area for additional information.

We have adjusted your return to update your tuition and education amounts for carryforward.

According to our records, you have unused federal tuition, education, and textbook amounts of $1,600 that you can carry forward to a future year.

According to our records, you have unused British Columbia tuition and education amounts of $1,600 that you can carry forward to a future year.

We are mailing to you separately your reassessment notices for two or more taxation years. The notice for the latest taxation year will show your combined total refund or balance due. We will send you any refund to which you are entitled after we have reassessed all your returns.

If you have any questions about your reassessment, please call our Enquiries service at 1-800-959-8281. If you need to contact another area of the Agency, see the telephone listings in the government section of your telephone book.

# Bogus audit 2009 by Internal Revenue Minister Gail Shea!

**Canada Revenue Agency / Agence du revenu du Canada**

**NOTICE OF REASSESSMENT**

Date: Jan 11, 2011    Name: WALLY MALLENBY    Tax year: 2009

At a later date, we may review your return to verify income you reported or deductions and credits you claimed. Keep all your slips, receipts, and other supporting documents in case we ask to see them.

**Explanation of changes and other important information**

This notice explains the results of our reassessment of your income tax return and any changes we may have made. Please refer to the "Summary" area for additional information.

We have adjusted your return to change the province of residence to Manitoba.

According to our records, you have unused federal tuition, education, and textbook amounts of $1,600 that you can carry forward to a future year.

According to our records, you have unused British Columbia tuition and education amounts of $1,800 that you can carry forward to a future year.

Based on available information at the beginning of 2011, your unused Tax-Free Savings Account (TFSA) contribution room is $15,000. For detailed information, visit My Account on our website at www.cra.gc.ca/myaccount. If you become a non-resident of Canada and later make a contribution to a TFSA, you may have to pay a tax. For more information, visit our website at www.cra.gc.ca/tfsa.

If you have any questions about your reassessment, please call our Enquiries service at 1-800-959-8281. If you need to contact another area of the Agency, see the telephone listings in the government section of your telephone book.

**Chapter 9**

**What can one expect from such a person as Internal Revenue Minister Gail Shea who had harassed the "little guy" for successfully suing the government!**

Who is this Gail Shea, anyway?

Well, when Gail Shea was Fisheries Minister she was a big supporter of the clubbing to death of baby seals!!

CANADA'S SHAME

The Canadian seal hunt : 'cruel, criminal, and out of control'

What an "arse" this Gail Shea is!

Anyone that supports killing baby seals – isn't worth "shite"!

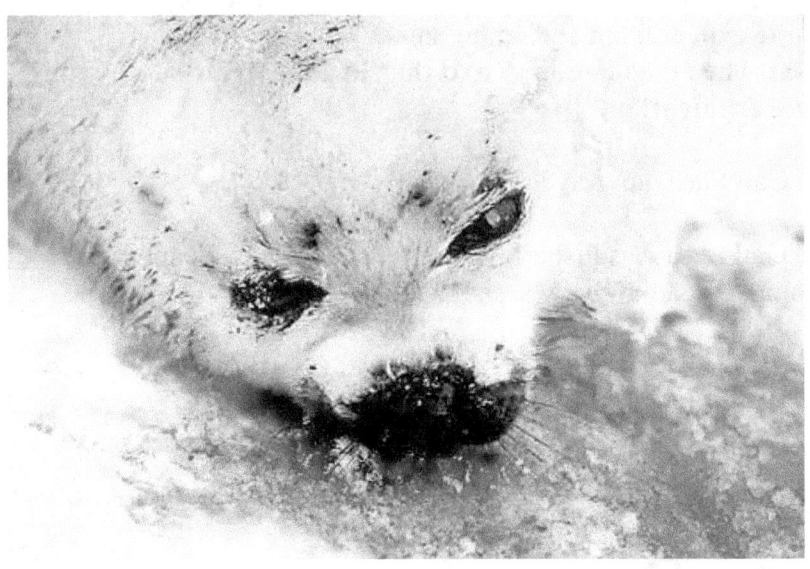

"Our hunt ... is sustainable, it's viable and it's humane" says Thomas Hedderson, the Minister of Fisheries and Aquaculture in Newfoundland and Labrador.

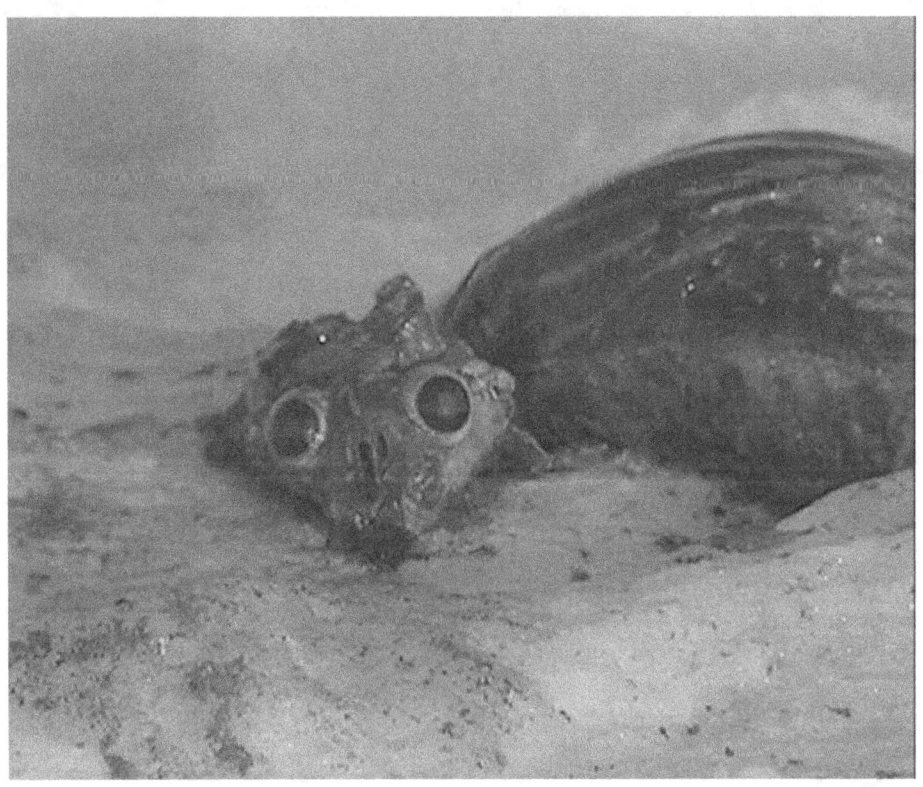

What does it feel like to see a baby seal clubbed to death in front of your eyes?

What does it feel like to be impaled on a boathook?

What does it feel like to be skinned alive?

Welcome to Canada!!

Why not write to Tom Hedderson and tell him what you think of his "humane" treatment of baby seals!

Tom Hedderson
402 Conception Bay Highway
P.O. Box 129
Holyrood, Newfoundland  A0A 2R0
Phone: (709) 229-0160
Fax: (709) 229-0169

Now do you see why the Mount Cashel scandal occurred in Newfoundland and the Whitbourne Center fiasco occurred in Newfoundland – because "air heads" like this Tom Hedderson thinks the baby seal hunt is "humane"?

**Chapter 10**

**Newfoundlanders have their own breed of corruption!**

Remember, the same person from British Columbia is also in charge of the Newfoundland income tax center where the second person in this story comes from.

That person in charge of the Newfoundland income tax center is Kerry Lynne Findlay, Canada's Internal Revenue Minister:

Kerry Lynne D. Findlay Q.C.
#202 - 5000 Bridge Street
Delta, British Columbia V4K 2K4
Tel: 604 940 8040
Fax: 604 940-8041
Email: Kerry-Lynne.Findlay@parl.gc.ca

So, a little more about Newfoundland, and their brand of corruption to give you a feel why Newfoundland felt free to harass the little guy's children as payback because he successfully sued Kerry Lynne Findlay's government [see below]!

Here's one example, Wally Andersen, Liberal Member of the House of Assembly:

*Long-time MHA Wally Andersen, who represents Torngat Mountains in Labrador, has been accused of overspending his spending constituency allowance limit by $243,244. Auditor general John Noseworthy said in his report that Andersen spent $591,644 over four years between 2003 and 2006. On June 27, 2006, Andersen was the third political figure to acknowledge he was being investigated.*

*Andersen was first elected in Torngat Mountains in 1996, was re-elected in 1999, and on Nov. 6, 2000, he was appointed parliamentary secretary to the premier on aboriginal affairs. On Feb. 13, 2001, he was appointed parliamentary secretary to the minister of Labrador and aboriginal affairs. About two years later, he was appointed minister of the same department.[1]*

How about this guy, Ed Byrne, former natural resources minister and government house leader

*Progressive Conservative cabinet minister Ed Byrne's resignation rocked Newfoundland and Labrador's political circles. Byrne, one of Premier Danny Williams most trusted colleagues, stepped down as house leader*

*and from his natural resources portfolio on June 21, 2006, after auditor general John Noseworthy expressed concern over the provincial legislature's financial records.*

*A day later, the full extent of the allegations was revealed in Noseworthy's report — Byrne had spent more than $326,000 more than his $31,500 limit on his constituency expenses, public money normally allotted for office rent, equipment and supplies. Noseworthy said Byrne signed and submitted claims for $358,142 during 2003 and 2004, with the paper trail pointing to Byrne's personal bank accounts.*

*Byrne was the first of four Newfoundland and Labrador politicians to be named in the audit scandal. Premier Danny Williams suspended Byrne from his position, and handed over his portfolio to Virginia Waters representative Kathy Dunderdale. But, Williams said Byrne would be welcome in cabinet if he is cleared.*

*Byrne was first elected to the house of assembly as a representative for Kilbride in 1993 and was re-elected in 1996, 1999 and 2003. He was leader of the Progressive Conservative Party of Newfoundland and Labrador and leader of the opposition from 1998 to 2001. He stepped down to make way for Williams to lead the party. Byrne served as minister of natural resources from November 2003 until he resigned.*[2]

Here's another example, Randy Collins, New Democrat Member of the House of Assembly:

*Labrador West representative Randy Collins was the second legislative member to acknowledge he was under investigation by John Noseworthy. When Noseworthy's report was released, it showed that Collins spent $295,418 more than his constituency allowance limit. Collins reportedly signed and filed claims totalling $525,018 over four years between 2003 and 2006. Collins was first elected to the house of assembly in 1999, and was re-elected in October 2003.*[3]

Here's one more example, Bill Murray, N.L. former director of financial operations

*Bill Murray sits at the center of the scandal, as he was the person in charge of the provincial house of assembly finances. He managed the constituency allowances that the auditor-general's investigation is now focused on. The auditor-general's report said the former director placed the orders, approved the invoices and paid the bills.*

*Not only were these orders untendered and with little documentation, payments were made for $69,000 in gold rings purchased from Unique*

*Keepsakes — a company Murray owned. The rings were reportedly purchased for legislative members, but few of them received the rings and some didn't know they existed. Liberal Leader Gerry Reid said he got one from Murray six years ago, and at least six of his 11-member caucus received rings.*

*Unique Keepsakes was paid about $170,000 of public money between 2001 and 2005, the audit said. The money came from various budgets of the house of assembly, including members' constituency allowances.*

*Murray was suspended from his position in June 2006.*[4]

And, what about this guy, Jim Walsh, former N.L. Liberal cabinet minister

*Jim Walsh was the fourth Newfoundland politician to acknowledge he was under investigation by the auditor general. John Noseworthy's report, detailing Walsh's constituency allowance claims, showed the former assembly member overspent his limit by $228,169. Walsh signed and filed claims totalling $289,169 between 2003 and 2004.*

*In the wake of the scandal, Walsh went on administrative leave from his post as federal Transportation Safety Board member. He will remain on paid leave until the situation is resolved.*

*Walsh served as tourism minister in the early 1990s for less than two years. He was forced to resign because of revelations of cash campaign donations on Feb. 22, 1994, but was vindicated in a later investigation. He returned to cabinet in February 2003, when then premier Roger Grimes appointed Walsh minister of works, services and transportation. He was a member of the house of assembly from 1989 until the October 2003 election, when Progressive Conservative Dianne Whalen defeated him.*[5]

And, these are the kind of people doing Ontario resident income tax returns?

Footnotes

1 - 5. Newfoundland and Labrador audit scandal: The players
CBC News, July 8, 2006

**The "little guy" successfully sued Kerry Lynne Findlay's government!**

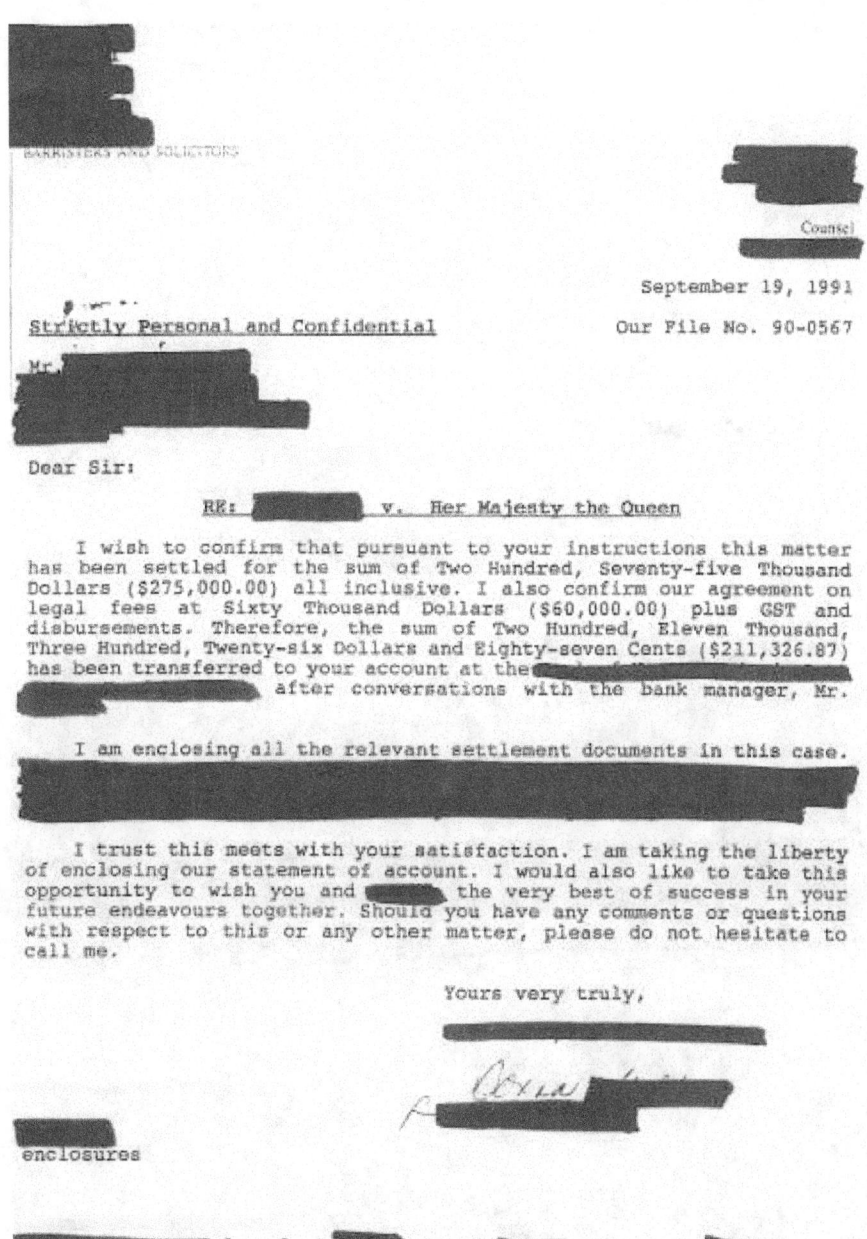

BARRISTERS AND SOLICITORS

Counsel

September 19, 1991

<u>Strictly Personal and Confidential</u>

Our File No. 90-0567

Mr.

Dear Sir:

RE: ▮▮▮▮▮ v. Her Majesty the Queen

I wish to confirm that pursuant to your instructions this matter
has been settled for the sum of Two Hundred, Seventy-five Thousand
Dollars ($275,000.00) all inclusive. I also confirm our agreement on
legal fees at Sixty Thousand Dollars ($60,000.00) plus GST and
disbursements. Therefore, the sum of Two Hundred, Eleven Thousand,
Three Hundred, Twenty-six Dollars and Eighty-seven Cents ($211,326.87)
has been transferred to your account at the ▮▮▮▮▮▮▮▮▮▮
▮▮▮▮▮▮▮▮▮▮▮▮▮ after conversations with the bank manager, Mr.

I am enclosing all the relevant settlement documents in this case.

I trust this meets with your satisfaction. I am taking the liberty
of enclosing our statement of account. I would also like to take this
opportunity to wish you and ▮▮▮▮ the very best of success in your
future endeavours together. Should you have any comments or questions
with respect to this or any other matter, please do not hesitate to
call me.

Yours very truly,

enclosures

Ottawa, Ontario ▮▮   Fax: (613) ▮▮▮   Telephone: (613) ▮▮▮

45

**The "little guy" successfully sued Kerry Lynne Findlay's government!**

No: T-1131-93

IN THE FEDERAL COURT OF CANADA
TRIAL DIVISION

BETWEEN:

███████,

and

Plaintiffs

AND:

HER MAJESTY THE QUEEN, ROYAL CANADIAN
MOUNTED POLICE and J.I. RANDLE.

Defendants

DECLARATION OF SETTLEMENT

The parties, by their counsel, hereby declare that the present case has now been settled, each party paying its own costs.

SIGNED in Montreal, this _____
day of September 1991

**The "little guy" successfully sued Kerry Lynne Findlay's government!**

Minister of Justice
and Attorney General of Canada

Ministre de la Justice
et Procureur général du Canada

A. Kim Campbell, P.C., Q.C., M.P./o.p., c.r., députée

OCT 15 1991

Mr. David Kilgour, M.P.
House of Commons
Ottawa, K1A 0A6

Dear Mr. Kilgour:

Thank you for your letter of August 21, 1991, concerning
Mr. ▓▓▓▓▓▓▓▓.

I have been informed that Treasury Board has now approved
the proposed settlement and that the cheque is being prepared.
The cheque as well as release documents will be forwarded to
Mr. ▓▓▓▓▓▓ counsel in the very near future, if this has not
already been done.

Yours sincerely,

A. Kim Campbell

RECEIVED - REÇU

OCT 18 1991

HOUSE OF COMMONS
Chambre des Communes

Ottawa, Canada K1A 0H8

**Chapter 11**

**And that's quite evident, here's one young fellow that received assessments / re-assessments from these Newfoundland "idiots" – all with different figures – and they still cheated the kid out of his College Credits!**

This young fellow reported this problem to Canada's Internal Revenue Minister Kerry Lynne Findlay:

*The Honourable Kerry-Lynne D. Findlay PC, QC, MP*
*Minister of National Revenue*
*7th Floor, 555 MacKenzie Avenue*
*Ottawa Ontario K1A 0L5*
*613-992-2957*
*Kerry-Lynne.Findlay@parl.gc.ca*
*stephen.harper@parl.gc.ca*

*The Honourable Kerry-Lynne D. Findlay PC, QC, MP*
*Minister of National Revenue*
*5000 Bridge Street, Suite 202*
*Delta, British Columbia V4K 2K4*
*Telephone: 604-940-8040*
*Fax: 604-940-8041*

*The Manager*
*REVENUE CANADA*
*St. John's Tax Center*
*290 Empire Avenue*
*St. John's, NEWFOUNDLAND A1B 3Z1*

*SEVERAL BLATANT ERRORS IN MY INCOME TAX SO-CALLED RE-ASSESSMENT BY YOUR ST. JOHN'S TAX CENTER*

*What is it with your St. John's Tax Center – my dad wants to know if they actually know what they are doing??*

*They have made several errors in their so-called Re-assessment???*

*I was cheated out of Federal Caregiver credit amounts [see attached].*

*I was cheated out of Ontario Provincial Caregiver credit amounts [see attached].*

*I was cheated out of Full-time Ontario student status & credit amounts [see attached].*

*Why do you have Ontario citizens send our Income tax forms to these apparent "idiots" in St. John's Tax Center in Newfoundland?*

*Your St. John's Tax Center isn't just "screwing around with me are they", as my dad calls it, especially since he successfully sued your government?*

*Signed,*

*The little guy's son and the little guy*

And what did the kid get back from Canada's Internal Revenue Minister Kerry Lynne Findlay?

Nothing but a bogus, con-game email!!

As Forrest Gump said "Stupid is as stupid does"!!

That seems to describe Canada's Internal Revenue Minister Kerry Lynne Findlay?

WHAT CAME BACK – A BOGUS, CON-GAME EMAIL??

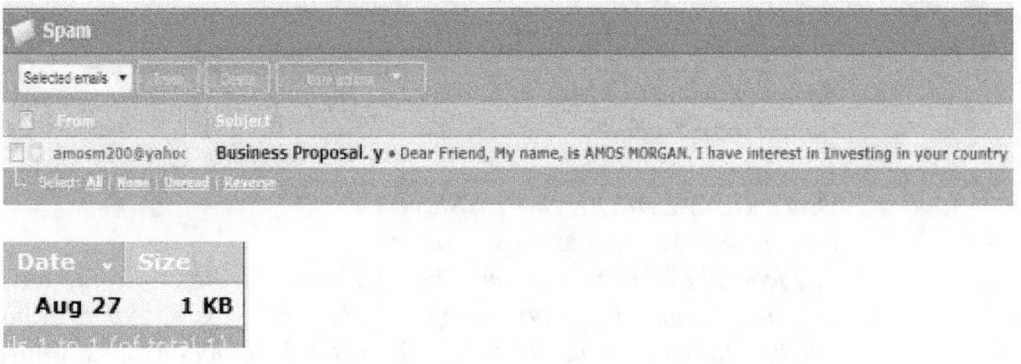

## Chapter 12

**Another person sends Internal Revenue Minister Kerry Lynne Findlay an email questioning errors made by her department, and they also get a "bogus, com-game" email in response from Kerry Lynne Findlay?**

Internal Revenue Minister Kerry Lynne Findlay apparently likes to send bogus, con-game emails to stifle questions about errors made by her department??

This young woman reported this problem to Canada's Internal Revenue Minister Kerry Lynne Findlay:

> *Kerry-Lynne D. Findlay PC, QC, MP*
> *Minister of National Revenue*
> *5000 Bridge Street, Suite 202*
> *Delta, British Columbia V4K 2K4*
> *Telephone: 604-940-8040*
> *Fax: 604-940-8041*
> *613-992-2957*
> *Kerry-Lynne.Findlay@parl.gc.ca*
> *stephen.harper@parl.gc.ca*

> *Based on my net income of $16,329.00 my proper medical expenses should total $489.87*

> *ONTARIO MEDICAL EXPENSES*
> *Line 5868 – Medical expenses for self*
> *The federal and provincial medical expenses you claim have to cover the same 12-month period ending in 2012, and must be expenses no one has claimed on a 2011 return. Your total medical expenses have to be more than either 3% of your net income (line 236 of your return) or $2,128, whichever is less.*

> *2012 NET INCOME $16,329 X 3% = $489.87*

*And not the $263 your Newfoundland St. John's Tax Center says!!*

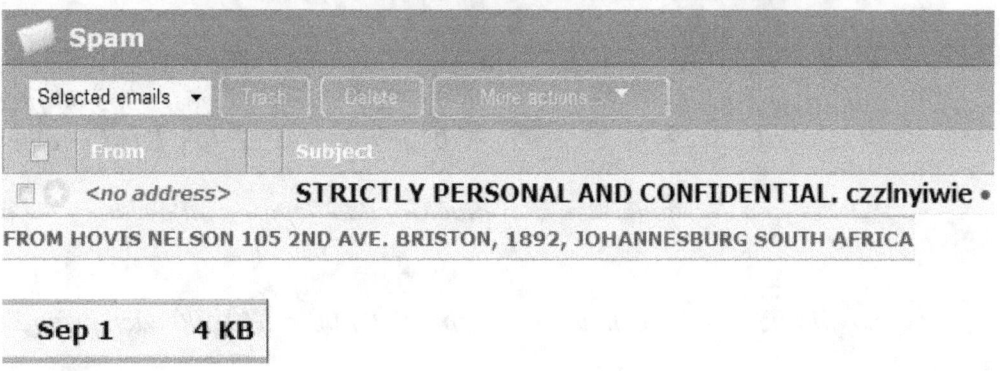

| enue  Agence du revenu du Canada | NOTICE OF ASSESSMENT | T451 E (13) |
| --- | --- | --- |
| | | 2 |

| Name | Social insurance No. | Tax year | Tax centre |
| --- | --- | --- | --- |
| 3 | | 2012 | St. John's NL A1B 3Z1 |

> As a result of a change to your net income, we have adjusted the allowable portions of your federal medical expenses from $309 to $263 and your Ontario medical expenses from $309 to $263.

*WHAT GIVES – YOUR NEWFOUNDLAND AGENTS CAN'T MULITPLY MY NET INCOME BY 3%???*

*Signed,*

*The little guy's daughter and the little guy*

And if you question that Kerry-Lynne Findlay as to why Ontario residents are forced to send their Income Tax Returns to the "Newfoundland "Idiots" who apparently are Cheating Ontario citizens out of income tax returns!

What does that "Bozo" Kerry-Lynne D. Findlay apparently do – she sends out more bogus, con-game emails??

WHAT CAME BACK ANOTHER BOGUS, CON-GAME EMAIL:

| ☐ Spam | |
| --- | --- |
| Selected emails ▾ | Trash  Delete  More actions ▾ |

| ☐ | From | Subject |
| --- | --- | --- |
| ☐ ○ | <no address> | **STRICTLY PERSONAL AND CONFIDENTIAL. czzlnyiwie** • |

FROM HOVIS NELSON 105 2ND AVE. BRISTON, 1892, JOHANNESBURG SOUTH AFRICA

| Sep 1 | 4 KB |
| --- | --- |

**Chapter 13**

**Yet another person sends Internal Revenue Minister Kerry Lynne Findlay an email questioning errors made by her department, and they too get a "bogus, com-game" email in response?**

Incredibly, Internal Revenue Minister Kerry-Lynne D. Findlay apparently sends out even more bogus, con-game emails to stifle questions about errors made by her department??

HERE'S ANOTHER ONTARIO CITIZEN CHEATED OUT OF ONTARIO TAX BENEFITS!!

> *Kerry-Lynne D. Findlay PC, QC, MP*
> *Minister of National Revenue*
> *5000 Bridge Street, Suite 202*
> *Delta, British Columbia V4K 2K4*
> *Telephone: 604-940-8040*
> *Fax: 604-940-8041*
> *613-992-2957*
> *Kerry-Lynne.Findlay@parl.gc.ca*
> *stephen.harper@parl.gc.ca*

> *Ms. Findlay,*

> *I finally got my 05 July, 2013 GST benefit payment, but the amount was only the basic annual amount of $265.00 [quarterly of $66.25]???????*

> *My dad looking at the rates for my situation of NO INCOME [see attached conformation], I should be getting the GST rate of at least $265.00 [basic credit] plus at least $139 [for someone with no income] = $404.00 per annum????*

> *Why is your Newfoundland Revenue Canada department cheating me out of the $139.00???*

> *So, for the amount I should be getting $404.00 = $101.00 each period!*

> *What your Revenue Canada department is doing is paying me a GST benefit of $66.25 per pay period [i.e., $265.00]!!!*

> *So would you kindly do this for me – and get your Revenue Canada Office in St. John's Newfoundland to correct their records and pay me at the proper rate of $404 per annum!!!*

IN RESPONSE TO QUESTIONING INTERNAL REVENUE MINISTER
KERRY-LYNNE FINDLAY, WHAT CAME BACK – YOU GUESSED IT –
ANOTHER BOGUS, CON-GAME EMAIL:

**Chapter 14**

**One more person sends Internal Revenue Minister Kerry-Lynne D. Findlay an email questioning errors made by her department, and they also get a "bogus, com-game" email in response?**

Internal Revenue Minister Kerry-Lynne D. Findlay apparently sends more bogus, con-game emails to stifle questions about her department??

HERE'S ANOTHER ONTARIO CITIZEN CHEATED OUT OF ONTARIO TAX BENEFITS!!

> *The Honourable Kerry-Lynne D. Findlay PC, QC, MP*
> *Minister of National Revenue*
> *5000 Bridge Street, Suite 202*
> *Delta, British Columbia V4K 2K4*
> *Telephone: 604-940-8040*
> *Fax: 604-940-8041*
> *613-992-2957*
> *Kerry-Lynne.Findlay@parl.gc.ca*
> *stephen.harper@parl.gc.ca*

> *Why am I being denied GST / HSTC payments by your Newfoundland Income Tax Center?*

> *According to your tax act, I am entitled to GST / HSTC payments?*

IN RESPONSE TO QUESTIONING REVENUE MINISTER KERRY-LYNNE FINDLAY, WHAT CAME BACK – YOU GUESSED IT – EVEN MORE BOGUS, CON-GAME EMAILS!!

THIS TIME 3 BOGUS, CON-GAME EMAILS!!!

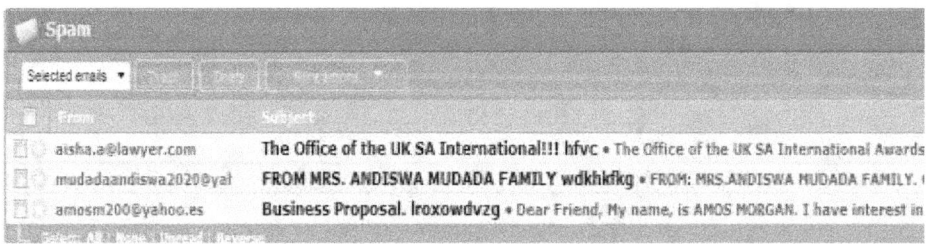

**Chapter 15**

**Setting Internal Revenue Minister Kerry-Lynne D. Findlay up, just like Pavlov's salivating dogs??**

Doesn't the apparent responses by Internal Revenue Minister Kerry-Lynne D. Findlay sending "bogus, con-game emails" every time someone questioned her department remind anyone of the classic S – R paradigm? [1]

Pavlov's salivating dogs??[2]

It appears to be the classic S – R response!!

Send Internal Revenue Minister Kerry-Lynne D. Findlay an email questioning errors made by her department [the S]!

And apparently get a "bogus, con-game" email in reply [the R]!

You would expect this from some Fascist government …

But one's not going to put up with this from a supposed Democratic government …

Where these government ministers are supposed to be accountable to the people!!

That's what representative government is all about!!

To test this hypothesis, the "little guy" sent Internal Revenue Minister Kerry-Lynne D. Findlay an email questioning her department:

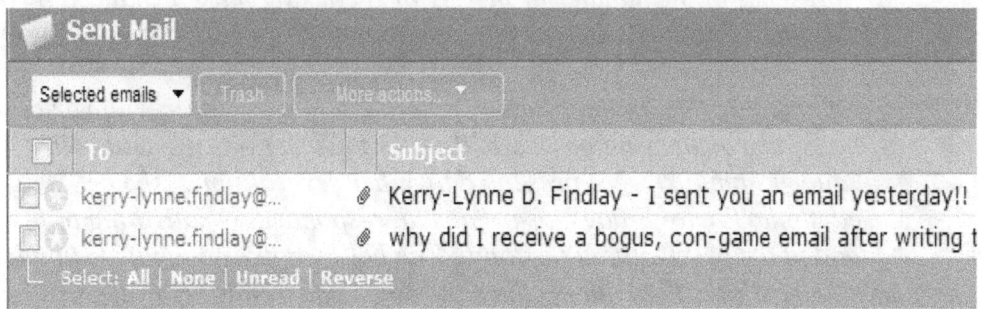

AND THE VERY NEXT DAY, A BOGUS, CON-GAME EMAIL WAS
RECEIVED APPARENTLY IN REPLY FROM INTERNAL REVENUE MINISTER
KERRY-LYNNE FINDLAY:

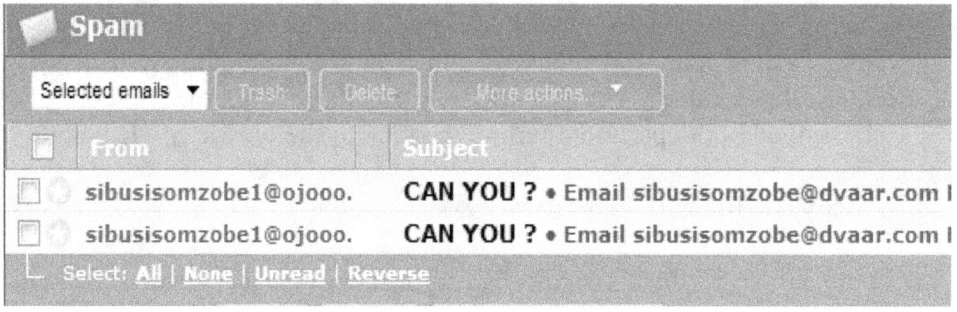

**Footnotes**

C1. Classical Conditioning (Pavlov)

*Classical conditioning is a reflexive or automatic type of learning in
which a stimulus acquires the capacity to evoke a response that was
originally evoked by another stimulus.*

*In the early twentieth century, Russian physiologist Ivan Pavlov did
Nobel prize-winning work on digestion. While studying the role of
saliva in dogs' digestive processes, he stumbled upon a phenomenon
he labeled "psychic reflexes." While an accidental discovery, he had
the foresight to see the importance of it. Pavlov's dogs, restrained in
an experimental chamber, were presented with meat powder and they
had their saliva collected via a surgically implanted tube in their
saliva glands. Over time, he noticed that his dogs who begin salivation
before the meat powder was even presented, whether it was by the
presence of the handler or merely by a clicking noise produced by the
device that distributed the meat powder.*

*Fascinated by this finding, Pavlov paired the meat powder with various
stimuli such as the ringing of a bell. After the meat powder and bell
(auditory stimulus) were presented together several times, the bell was
used alone. Pavlov's dogs, as predicted, responded by salivating to the
sound of the bell (without the food). The bell began as a neutral stimulus
(i.e. the bell itself did not produce the dogs' salivation). However, by
pairing the bell with the stimulus that did produce the salivation response,
the bell was able to acquire the ability to trigger the salivation response.
Pavlov therefore demonstrated how stimulus-response bonds (which some
consider as the basic building blocks of learning) are formed. He
dedicated much of the rest of his career further exploring this finding.*

*In technical terms, the meat powder is considered an unconditioned stimulus (UCS) and the dog's salivation is the unconditioned response (UCR). The bell is a neutral stimulus until the dog learns to associate the bell with food. Then the bell becomes a conditioned stimulus (CS) which produces the conditioned response (CR) of salivation after repeated pairings between the bell and food.*

2. Pavlov, I. P. (1927). *Conditioned Reflexes: An Investigation of the Physiological Activity of the Cerebral Cortex*. Translated and Edited by G. V. Anrep. London: Oxford University Press

**Chapter 16**

**Let's repeat Pavlov's salivating dogs experiment with Internal Revenue Minister Kerry-Lynne D. Findlay just to confirm initial results??**

One has to repeat an experiment to confirm results!!

As such, the "little guy" tested his theory by sending Kerry-Lynne D. Findlay another email questioning her department!!

Low and behold, another bogus, con-game email – eureka the experiment was a success - Kerry-Lynne D. Findlay apparently acted just like Pavlov's salivating dogs??

AGAIN, THE ONLY PERSON SENT AN EMAIL QUESTIONG HER DEPARTMENT WAS TO INTERNAL REVENUE MINISTER KERRY-LYNNE FINDLAY:

INCREDIBLY, THREE OTHER BOGUS, CON-GAME EMAIL
APPARENTLY IN REPLY CAME FROM INTERNAL REVENUE MINISTER
KERRY-LYNNE FINDLAY:

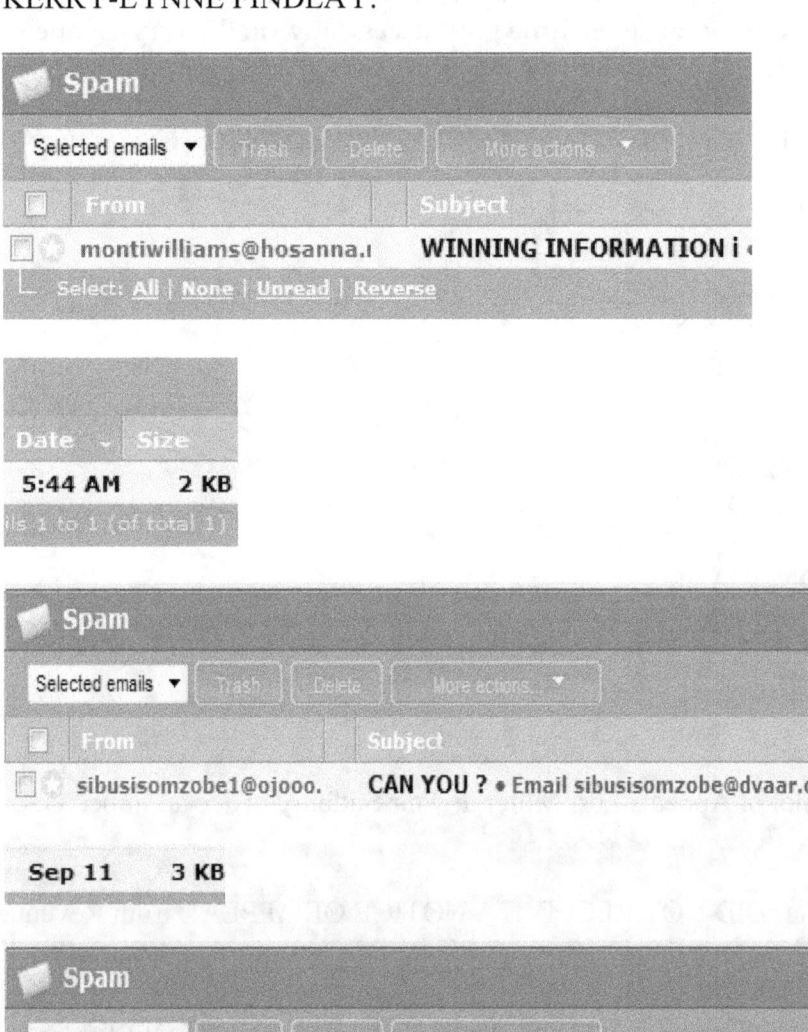

**Chapter 17**

**Internal Revenue Minister Kerry-Lynne D. Findlay is still screwing with the little guy's daughter because the little guy successfully sued Kerry-Lynne Findlay's government!**

September 10, 2014

J. Paul Dubé, Taxpayers' Ombudsman
Office of the Taxpayers' Ombudsman
Canada Revenue
724 – 50 O'Connor Street
Ottawa ON K1P 6L2

Lori Miller, L'idiote
Chief of Appeals
Canada Revenue
1050 Notre Dame Avenue
Sudbury ON  P3A 5C1

File # 18900

Hello,

Is your Chief of Appeals Lori Miller at your Sudbury office an imbecilic or just plain stupid?

My daughter DID NOT RECEIVE A NOTICE OF APPEAL from Revenue Canada in St. John's Newfoundland where some Ontarians have to send their forms!!!!!

My daughter appealed asking that she be sent a NOTICE OF ASSESSMENT!!!

And that idiot says she is over the 90 days from the Notice of Assessment?????

Listen idiots, my daughter never received a NOTICE OF ASSESSMENT so how could she be past the 90 days cut-off???

Plain bloody stupid or lazy – is that it – too lazy to do your job Lori Miller – and have Revenue Canada send her a NOTICE OF ASSESSMENT as she requested??

Thanks,

The little guy and his daughter

## Chapter 18

**Internal Revenue Minister Kerry-Lynne D. Findlay is still screwing with the little guy's daughter because the little guy successfully sued Kerry-Lynne Findlay's government!**

September 22, 2014

J. Paul Dubé, Taxpayers' Ombudsman
ATTENTION DEREK GLEDHILL
Office of the Taxpayers' Ombudsman
Canada Revenue
724 – 50 O'Connor Street
Ottawa ON K1P 6L2

File # 18900

Hello,

Here's another game being played by Internal Revenue Minister Kerry-Lynne D. Findlay:

Kerry-Lynne D. Findlay, P.C., Q.C., M.P.
Minister of National Revenue, 7th Floor
555 MacKenzie Avenue
Ottawa, Ontario, Canada K1A 0L5
Kerry-Lynne.Findlay@parl.gc.ca

Instead of sending my daughter a NOTICE OF ASSESSMENT, that "Pavlov dog" plays more silly games, as attached.

Maybe you can help my daughter receive a Notice of Assessment as she has NEVER RECEIVED A NOTICE OF ASSESSMENT from Internal Revenue Minister Kerry-Lynne D. Findlay!

Thanks,

The little guy and his daughter

**Chapter 19**

**Internal Revenue Minister Kerry-Lynne D. Findlay is still screwing with the little guy's son because he successfully sued Kerry-Lynne Findlay's government!**

The little guy's son writes to Internal Revenue Minister Kerry-Lynne D. Findlay about her agent G.C. Murphy trying to cheat him out of full-time student status????

His letter goes unanswered?

> The Honourable Kerry-Lynne D. Findlay PC, QC, MP
> Minister of National Revenue
> 7th Floor, 555 MacKenzie Avenue
> Ottawa ON K1A 0L5
> 613-992-2957
> Kerry-Lynne.Findlay@parl.gc.ca
> stephen.harper@parl.gc.ca
>
> Ms. Findlay,
>
> CHEATED OUT OF FULL-TIME STUDENT STATUS:
>
> The little guy's son finally received his 2012 tax assessment and Kerry-Lynne D. Findlay's agent G.C. Murphy is trying to cheat him out of full-time student status????
>
> *Full-time college program*
> *T2022A TUITION AMOUNT – $1,654.31*
> *4 MONTHS – COLUMN C [EDUCATION AMOUNT] = $400 X 4 = $1,200*
> *4 MONTHS – COLUMN C [TEXTBOOK AMOUNT] = $65 X 4 = $260.00*
> *TOTAL AMOUNT   $3,114.31*
>
> This, however, appears NO WHERE on the 2012 tax assessment [see below].
>
> In fact, Kerry-Lynne D. Findlay's agent G.C. Murphy cheats him by saying that for his educational amount he was to receive $0 credit – because the bloody moron G.C. Murphy classes the boy's full-time study as p/t????
>
> What a moron!!
>
> As such, the little guy's son is being cheated out of $3,114.31 in full-time student educational credits by Kerry-Lynne D. Findlay and her agent G.C. Murphy?
>
> This educational full-time student credit would have reduced the boy's net income?

Did Kerry-Lynne D. Findlay do anything about this cheat?

No way, not by the time of publication!!

Another good-for-nothing Canadian politician??

Because this evidence was sent by registered mail directly to G.C. Murhpy and she ignored it proves that she was out to cheat the little guy's son as Internal Revenue Minister Kerry-Lynne Findlay's harassment for the little guy's successful suit of her government!

PROOF THAT FINDLAY'S AGENT G.C. MURPHY RECEIVED PROOF OF FULL-TIME STUENT STATUS!!

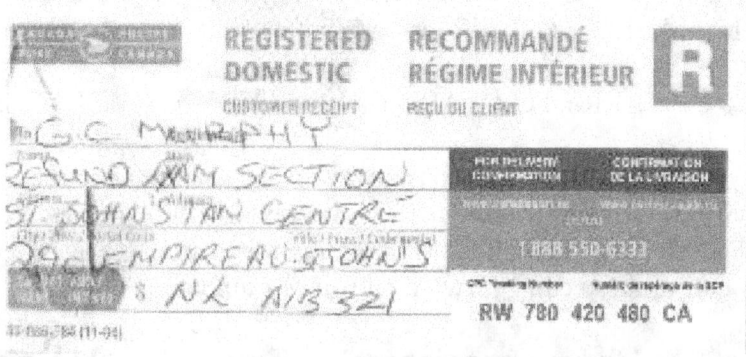

PROOF THAT FINDLAY'S AGENT G.C. MURPHY LIED AND CLASSED THE EDUCATION AS PART-TIME TO THE LOTTLE GUY'S SON OUT OF FULL-TIME STUDENT STATUS!!

| ■◆■ | Canada Revenue Agency | Agence du revenu du Canada | NOTICE OF ASSESSMENT | | | T451 E (13) 2 |
|---|---|---|---|---|---|---|
| Date Aug 12. 2013 | Name | | Social Insurance No. | Tax year 2012 | Tax centre St. John's NL A1B 3Z1 | |

Based on the information provided, we have adjusted your Ontario claim for the part-time education amount to $0, which is the maximum you can claim.

However, that's not all the lies that Kerry-Lynne D. Findlay's agent G.C. Murphy did in the little guy's son 2012 tax assessment?

CHEATED OUT OF CARRY FORWARD EDUCATIONAL AMOUNTS:

In previous tax year assessments, there has always been a section about carrying forward federal and provincial education amounts [tuitions, text books] – however NO WHERE in in the little guy's son 2012 tax assessment by Findlay's agent G.C. Murhpy is there any mention of these carry forward educations amounts?

Is Findlay's agent G.C. Murhpy also trying to cheat Terry Mallenby's son out of these carry forward educations amounts?

However, that's not all the lies that Kerry-Lynne D. Findlay's agent G.C. Murphy did in the little guy's son 2012 tax assessment?

CHEATED OUT OF CARRY FORWARD MOVING EXPENSES:

In a letter dated July, 2013 by Kerry-Lynne D. Findlay's agent G.C. Murhpy he clearly states that the little guy's son will have $7,421.00 in moving expenses to be carried forward for next year [see below]?

However, NO WHERE on the little guy's son 2013 tax assessment by Findlay's agent G.C. Murhpy is this carry-forward amount of $7,421.00 mentioned??

It appears that Findlay's agent G.C. Murhpy is trying to cheat the little guy's son out of this amount too??

**However, NO WHERE on the little guy's son 2013 tax assessment by Findlay's agent G.C. Murhpy is this carry-forward amount of $7,421.00 mentioned??**

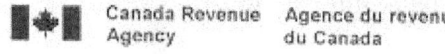 Canada Revenue    Agence du revenu
Agency            du Canada

Tax Centre
St. John's NL  A1B 3Z1

                                                    July 26, 2013

                                                    Account Number

Dear Sir:

Re:   Income Tax and Benefit Return for 2012

We acknowledge receipt of your reply to our letter dated July 9,
2013.

Based on the information provided we have accepted your claim for
moving expenses of $9,143.

                              The remaining amount of $7,421
can be carried forward to your 2013 income tax return and claimed
against income earned from the new work location.

Yours sincerely,

G.C. Murphy
Refund Examination Section
Canada Revenue Agency, St. John's Tax Centre
290 Empire Avenue, St. John's NL A1B 3Z1

Enclosure(s)

**Chapter 20**

**The next thing the little guy's son knows there's another "con-game" email from Internal Revenue Minister Kerry-Lynne Findlay trying to get the boy's bank information?**

"Con-game" email trying to get the boy's bank information?

BMO Accounts , security alert for : thegoodones@live.ca

BMO ALERTS (stfu09@cox.net)  Add to contacts  16/08/2013
To: thegood

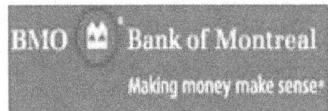

Dear BMO Customer,

We are currently performing regular maintenance of our systems. Your account has been selected for this maintenance, because of long periods of inactivity.

For security purposes, accounts inactive for long periods of time will be disabled. In order to prevent this from hapening you need to login to your account.

To access your account please click here

Please Note:
If we do not receive any action within 24 hours, we will assume this account is no longer being used and it will be disabled. Protecting the security of your BMO account is our primary concern, and we apologize for any inconvenience this may cause. Sincerely,
Abbey BMO Review Department

As the dad says, anything is possible with these louts, especially when the leader of the pack, Canadian Prime Minister Stephen Harper is pictured in a "Gestapo uniform"?

*[see picture of Stephen Harper in gestapo clothes]*
*http://fredericks-artworks.blogspot.ca/2012_06_01_archive.html*

**Chapter 21**

**Internal Revenue Minister Kerry-Lynne D. Findlay is still screwing with the little guy's son because the little guy successfully sued Kerry-Lynne Findlay's government!**

September 26, 2014

J. Paul Dubé, Taxpayers' Ombudsman
Office of the Taxpayers' Ombudsman
Canada Revenue
724 – 50 O'Connor Street
Ottawa ON K1P 6L2

Lori Miller, L'idiote
Chief of Appeals
Canada Revenue
1050 Notre Dame Avenue
Sudbury ON  P3A 5C1

File # 18901

Hello,

Is your Chief of Appeals Lori Miller at your Sudbury office an imbecilic or just plain stupid?

His appeal / objection is a desire to receive a new Notice of Assessment with the proper amounts in it for his unused provincial and federal unused tuition amounts!

HIS  NOTICE OF ASSESSMENT WAS RECEIVED JULY 24, 2014 – THE APPEAL WAS AUGUST 2, 2014!!!

DOES THAT MORON LORI MILLER KNOW HOW TO COUNT???

How can that idiot Lori Miller say my son was past 90 days from the Notice of Assessment [see below]?????

What is Lori Miller – too lazy to send my son a new Notice of Assessment with the proper amounts in it for his unused provincial and federal unused tuition amounts??

Thanks,

The little guy and his son

Appeals Division
Sudbury ON  P3A 5C1

September 23, 2014

Account Number

Dear Sir:

Re:  Your objection for 2013 filed August 24, 2014

This is to inform you that we have received your objection.

Since you filed the objection before the Notice of Determination
was issued, the Appeals Division cannot accept your objection.

For an objection to be valid, you have to file it within 90 days
from the mailing date of the Notice of Determination. The Notice
of Determination was issued on September 05, 2014

Should you have any questions, please do not hesitate to contact
the Eastern Appeals Intake Centre at (705) 671-0238 or toll free
at 1-866-242-3161 or by toll free fax at 1-866-443-4955.

Yours sincerely,

Lori Miller
Chief of Appeals
Sudbury Tax Services Office
Canada Revenue Agency

Sudbury Tax Services Office
1050 Notre Dame Avenue
Sudbury ON  P3A 5C1

Local :          705-671-0238
Toll Free :      1-866-242-3161
Fax :            705-671-0388
Web site :       www.cra.gc.ca

**Chapter 22**

**Maybe Internal Revenue Minister Kerry-Lynne Findlay and her internal revenue gang are just too stoned or too illiterate to correct their screwing with the little guy's son and daughter?**

August 8, 2014

Kerry-Lynne D. Findlay, P.C., Q.C., M.P.
Minister of National Revenue
7th Floor
555 MacKenzie Avenue
Ottawa ON K1A 0L5
Kerry-Lynne.Findlay@parl.gc.ca

We have written to you for two years now without reply – your St. John's Newfoundland tax return office has not cited my son's unused provincial and federal unused tuition amounts in his assessment for two years now and my daughter was not sent a notice of assessment?

Why is that??

Too stupid to reply???

Just plain ignorant???

Or, just another "scum-bag" psychopath politician:

Dr. Dutton from Oxford's Magdalen College speaks about psychopaths finding their way into politics cited in Michael Posner's article, published in the Globe and Mail on Friday, Oct. 26 2012:

*It's not surprising that politics attracts a disproportionate number of psychopaths. "Politicians must be self-confident, fearless, very good at persuasion and manipulation, and be mentally tough to deal with crises," he says. "One senior British MP – he shall remain nameless – told me the only way to see who was stabbing you in the back was to see their reflection in the eyes of the person stabbing you in the front."*

Then again, maybe you are too "stoned" in British Columbia to reply:

*B.C. official pot capital of Canada*
*by: Stephanie Mamayson, Gauntlet News*

*Pot. Weed. Grass. Mary-Jane. Ganja. Wacky Tobacky. Whatever name it goes by, cannabis is one of the drugs of choice among many British Columbians.*

We have also again written to your St. John's Newfoundland tax return office agent M.A. JOY about this purposeful error on my son's "Notice of Assessment" and the fact that my daughter did not receive a notice of assessment:

**M.A. JOY**
Refund examination Center
290 Empire Avenue
St. John's NL A1B 3Z1

This M.A. JOY doesn't reply either?

Maybe the problem is M.A. JOY just can't read in Newfoundland – is that the problem?

*More than half of the populations of Newfoundland and Labrador (56.8%) had literacy scores below Level 3 [Employment and Social Development Canada stats].*

Regards,

The little guy

cc. Stephen Harper, Prime Minister
1600 - 90th Avenue SW Suite A-203
Calgary, AlbertaT2V 5A8
Telephone: 403-253-7990
Fax: 403-253-8203
stephen.harper@parl.gc.ca
stephen.harper.c1@parl.gc.ca

cc. Justin Trudeau, Liberal MP
529 Jarry Street East Suite 302
Montréal, QuébecH2P 1V4
Telephone: 514-277-6020
Fax: 514-277-3454
justin.trudeau@parl.gc.ca
justin.trudeau.c1@parl.gc.ca

**Chapter 23**

**An open letter to Terry Mallenby**
Revenue Ombudsman files #18900 and #18901

*Terry Mallenby, BA, BSW, MA*
*former federal peace officer*
*former Classification Officer BC Maximum Security Penitentiary*
*former Classification Officer BC Medium Security Mountain Prison*
*former Probation Officer NFLD Social Services Department*
*former Facility Operations Manager Whitbourne Youth Secure Custody*

*Dear Mr. Mallenby,*

*You are absolutely right.*

*The little guy successfully sued my government.*

*As payback, I have and my department has harassed his children ever since denying them Unused Federal and Provincial tuition grants to reduce the income tax they owe.*

*And since I run the Office of the Taxpayers' Ombudsman office, they will have no satisfaction complaining about my harassment of the little guy's children!*

*Does this make me a bad person?*

*Signed*

*Kerry Lynne Findlay*
*Canada's Internal Revenue Minister*

## TERRY W. MALLENBY RESUME

*Former State Facility Operations Manager – Secure Custody Young Offenders*
*Former Classification Officer – Maximum Security Adult Penitentiary*
*Former Federal Manpower Immigration Counselor*
*Act/Dist. Manager Child Protection Social Services*
*Cited in National Library of Medicine*
*Listed in City University of Hong Kong Library*
*Referenced in Bodleian Law Library*
*Listed in Loyola University Chicago Library*
*Referenced in Cambridge University Library*
*Cited in Metropolitan Toronto Reference Library*
*Published Doctoral Dissertation - UMI*
*"Expert Witness" Supreme Court of B.C. [1973]*

**The BC Penitentiary, an imposing granite fortress along
the main thoroughfare between Coquitlam and New Westminster.**

*The Officer Down Memorial - dedicated to each and every law enforcement officer
who have had their life taken while in the performance of their duties.*
***Classification Officer Mary Steinhauser***
***Department of Corrections***
***Cause of Death: Gunfire***
***End of Watch: June 11, 1975***
***Age: 32***

*Mary Steinhauser was shot to death as guards rushed prisoners holding her hostage.*
*She was employed at the British Columbia Penitentiary at the time of her death.*

**National Center for Biotechnology Information, U.S. National Library of Medicine**

Facilitating the disappearance of perceptual error to the Poggendorff illusion.
Mallenby TW. Lang Speech. 1976 Apr-Jun;19(2):193-9.
PMID: 1018566 [PubMed - indexed for MEDLINE]

The personal space of hard-of-hearing children after extended contact with 'normals'.
Mallenby TW, Mallenby RG.
Br J Soc Clin Psychol. 1975 Sep;14(3):253-7.
PMID: 1182405 [PubMed - indexed for MEDLINE]

The effect of extended contact with "normals" on the social behavior of hard-of-hearing children.
Mallenby TW.
J Soc Psychol. 1975 Feb;95(First Half):137-8.
PMID: 1113519 [PubMed - indexed for MEDLINE]

Effect of discussion on reduction of magnitude of Poggendorff illusion.
Mallenby TW.
Percept Mot Skills. 1974 Oct;39(2):787-91.
PMID: 4453496 [PubMed - indexed for MEDLINE]

Personal space: projective and direct measures with institutionalized mentally retarded children.
Mallenby TW.
J Pers Assess. 1974 Feb;38(1):28-31.
PMID: 4592504 [PubMed - indexed for MEDLINE]

A note on perceived self-acceptance of institutionalized mentally retarded (IMR) children.
Mallenby TW.
J Genet Psychol. 1973 Sep;123(1st Half):171-2.
PMID: 4593476 [PubMed - indexed for MEDLINE]

**City University of Hong Kong Library**

A bibliography of research on spatial and social behaviour / compiled by
Terry W. Mallenby, Ruth G. Roberts.
Thomas Todd Press, c1973.
Shatin Storage, Call # C0237118

**Oxford University, Bodleian Libraries:**

Canada's criminal justice system : guilty until proved innocent : case study from Cour Supérieure en matière de faillite, Palais de Justice (Montreal), File #500-11-002290-894
Terry Wallice Mallenby
Publication Date: 1990
Aleph System Number: 010456749

Nicole Bomberg, an investigator with the Ant-Discrimination [sic] Directorate of the Public Service Commission of Canada purposefully lies in a letter dated 26 August, 1983 to hide the fact that false murder charge statements were made ..
Terry Wallice Mallenby
Publication Date: 1990
Aleph System Number: 010458715

Alberta crown agent RAE Kubik's legacy to Canada : more fabricated statements by government agent(s)
Terry Wallice Mallenby.
Publication Date: 1999
Aleph System Number: 013699710

Incidents of physical assault against child-abuse investigation workers : the nature of child-abuse protection legislation as a possible reason for such incidents
 Further information: some Canadian provincial examples of internal policies attempting to deal with such incidents: placing the trend of such incidents in a theoretical perspective, by Terry W. Mallenby
Author:Mallenby, Terry W., 1947-
Publisher Details: Thesis (doctoral)--Kensington University, 1994
Subjects:Child abuse -- Law and legislation -- United States ; Child abuse -- Law and legislation -- Canada; Child abuse -- United States -- Investigation ; Child abuse -- Canada -- Investigation ; Social workers -- Crimes against
 Aleph System Number: 011403458

## Loyola University Chicago Library

"$275,000 of taxpayer's money wasn't enough!" : the federal government of Canada conspiracy
Terry Wallice Mallenby.
Wallice Institute of Psychometric Assessment, 1999.
Subjects:Political persecution--Canada--Case studies.
Judicial error--Canada--Case studies.
False testimony--Canada--Case studies.
Misconduct in office--Canada--Case studies.
Location: Cudahy Main Stacks
Call Number: KE9440 .M23 T86 1999

## Cambridge University Library

Complete discharge from bankruptcy, including preferred Canadian and Quebec student loans, due to false statements by the Royal Canadian Mounted Police
Terry Wallice Mallenby
Institute of Psychometric Assessment, 1990.
Subject(s):
Bankruptcy -- Canada.
Royal Canadian Mounted Police.
Tort liability of police -- Canada.
Call # 1992.11.299

Dealing with a violent work environment : internal policies and legislation dealing with physical assault and other threats against child protective social workers / Terry W. Mallenby.
Distributed by Institute of Psychometric Assessment, Applied Studies & Investigative Research, 1994.
ISBN: 0969594402
Subject(s):
Abused children -- Services for -- United States.
Abused children -- Services for -- Canada.
Social workers -- Crimes against -- United States.
Social workers -- Crimes against -- Canada.
Call # 1995.10.275

Child abuse: a beginning social worker's understanding and use of the DSM-III-R and three reactive mental disorders following child abuse : reactive attachment disorder, post-traumatic stress disorder, and adjustment disorder
Terry W. Mallenby
Distributed by Instiutute of Psychometric Assessment, 1994.
Subject(s):
Adjustment disorders in children.
Attachment behaviour in children.
Child abuse.
Post-traumatic stress disorder in children.
Call # 1998.10.411

## Metropolitan Toronto Reference Library

How to make staff safe: how to reduce labour-management conflict: how to reduce staff grievances
By Terry W. Mallenby
Year: 1997, Book, 2 v.
 Subjects:
•Child abuse--Investigation.
•Child welfare workers--Training of.
•Child welfare--Administration.
•Social work administration.
•Social work with children--Administration.
•Social workers--Training of.
•Violence in the workplace.
•Violence--Forecasting.
2 copies
Reference only - not holdable
ISBN: 0969594402
Call # 361.3068 M12 1997 V. 1
Call #361.3068 M12 1997 V. 2

**WorldCat is the world's largest library catalog**

Cognitive development: the functional aspect of symbolization and language,
by Terry W Mallenby
Winnipeg, S. Evans, ©1973.
Database: WorldCat

Personal space : direct measurement techniques with hard-of-hearing children
by Terry W Mallenby
Publisher: Sage Publications, 1974.
Database: WorldCat

The effect of verbal mediation on the reduction of error to the Poggendorff illusion
by Terry W Mallenby
Publication: Bulletin of the Psychonomic Society, v5 n2 (19750205): 170-172
Database: CrossRef

Teach your child to read : a simple method for parents and educators
by Terry W Mallenby
Institute of Applied Studies, 1984.
Database: WorldCat

The relative effectiveness of whole- and part-task simulators
by Terry Mallenby
Institute of Applied Studies, 1984.
Database: WorldCat

Using the minnesota multiphasic personality inventory (MMPI) to determine the suitability of an inmate for parole, release or temporary absence.
by Terry Mallenby
Institute of Applied Studies 1984.
Database: WorldCat

When the "baby-boom" cohort reaches 65 : will it be social chaos or a carefully planned transition : an introductory research proposal
by Terry W Mallenby
Institute of Psychometric Assessment & Applied Studies, 1986.
Database: WorldCat

Quality assurance in medical/health care utilizing and incorporating three methods of evaluation: process, setting and outcome : an introduction to assessing medical/health care by means of a conceptual "process matrix" : with special reference to acute care and chronic care hospitals
by Terry W Mallenby
Institute of Psychometric Assessment and Applied Studies, 1986.
Database: WorldCat

Human rights violations in Canada : individual being denied employment with the Federal Government of Canada due to false "murder charge" statements made by M.J. Hauser of the Correctional Service of Canada and by Nicole Bomberg of the Public Service Commission of Canada : (continuing case study from Cour supérieure en matière de faillite, Palais de justice, Montréal, File #500-11-002290-894) : can the new Solicitor General of Canada, Hon. Pierre Cadiuex, correct the damage and have this individual re-hired by the Federal Government of Canada?
by Terry Wallice Mallenby
Institute of Psychometric Assessment, Applied Studies and Investigative Research, 1990
Database: WorldCat

Complete discharge from bankruptcy, including preferred Canadian and Quebec student loans, due to false statements by the Royal Canadian Mounted Police...
by Terry Mallenby
Institute of Psychometric Assessment, 1990.
Database: WorldCat

Dealing with a violent work environment : internal policies and legislation dealing with physical assault and other threats against child protective social workers
by Terry W Mallenby
Institute of Psychometric Assessment, Applied Studies & Investigative Research, 1994
Database: WorldCat

Child abuse : a beginning social worker's understanding and use of the DSM-III-R and three reactive mental disorders following child abuse : reactive attachment disorder, post-traumatic stress disorder, and adjustment disorder
by Terry Wallice Mallenby
Institute of Psychometric Assessment, 1994.
Database: WorldCat

Incidents of physical assault against child-abuse investigation workers: the nature of child-abuse protection legislation as a possible reason for such incidents
by Terry W Mallenby
Thesis/dissertation : Thesis/dissertation
Publisher: Ann Arbor : UMI, 1994.
Database: WorldCat

R.C.M.P. Sgt. John ("Jack") Thomas Randle's legacy to Canada.
by Terry W Mallenby
Institute of Psychometric Assessment, Applied Studies & Investigative Research, 1996
Database: WorldCat

Complete discharge from bankruptcy including preferred student loans due to Royal Canadian Mounted Police harassment : a most unusual case of bankruptcy.
by Terry W Mallenby
Wallice Institute of Psychometric Assessment, 1997
Database: WorldCat

How to make staff safe: how to reduce labour-management conflict : how to reduce staff grievances
by Terry W Mallenby
Wallice Institute of Psychometric Assessment & Applied Studies, 1997?
Database: WorldCat

Human rights violations in Canada by federal agents of the Canadian Human Rights Anti-Discrimination Agency of the Public Service Commission of Canada.
by Terry W Mallenby
Wallice Institute of Psychometric Assessment, 1997.
Database: WorldCat

The Newfoundland Department of Social Services is the worst department this author has ever read about.
by Terry W Mallenby
Wallice Institute of Psychometric Assessment, 1997.
Database: WorldCat

"Is he Canada's example of another Mark Furman : R.C.M.P. Sgt. John ("Jack") Thomas Randle purposefully committed lies, fabricated evidence, made false statements & committed illegal acts!"
by Terry W Mallenby
Wallice Institute of Psychometric Assessment & Applied Studies, 1997
Database: WorldCat

One of the worst social service departments this author has ever seen; receiving a lot of bad press for ignoring cruelly abused children and staff concerns about safety
by Terry W Mallenby
Wallice Institute of Psychometric Assessment, 1997
Database: WorldCat

Is it an example of unethical behavior by two psychiatrists? What do you think?.
by Terry W Mallenby
Wallice Institute of Psychometric Assessment, 1997.
Database: WorldCat

Judge John Gomery's inappropriate comments based on lies, false statements, fabricated statements & illegal acts by R.C.M.P. Sgt. John Thomas Randle.
by Terry W Mallenby
Wallice Institute of Psychometric Assessment & Applied Studies, 1998.
Database: WorldCat

Can police harassment involving illegal acts, false statements and fabricated evidence lead to a diagnosis of post-traumatic stress disorder sufficient to approve permanent disability pension?.
by Terry W Mallenby
Wallice Institute of Psychometric Assessment & Applied Studies, 1998.
Database: WorldCat

Is it an example of unethical behavior by a psychologist? What do you think?
by Terry W Mallenby
Wallice Institute of Psychometric Assessment & Applied Studies, 1998.
Database: WorldCat

Royal Canadian Mounted Police officers Sgt. John ("Jack") Thomas Randle's & Cpl. Jackett's legacy to Canada.
by Terry W Mallenby
Wallice Institute of Psychometric Assessment, 1998.
Database: WorldCat

Canadian anti-discriminate [sic] directorate and Canadian public service staff Nicole Bomberg's legacy to Canada.
by Terry W Mallenby
Wallice Institute of Psychometric Assessment, 1998.
Database: WorldCat

Federal government of Canada staff lies cost Canadian taxpayers plenty!
by Terry W Mallenby
Wallice Institute of Psychometric Assessment, 1998.
Database: WorldCat

Canadian anti-discrimination directorate and Canadian public service staff Lorisa Stein's legacy to Canada.
by Terry W Mallenby
Wallice Institute of Psychometric Assessment, 1998.
Database: WorldCat

Kofi Annan, Secretary General of the United Nations and Mary Robinson, the Human Rights Commissioner : their legacy to the world

by Terry W Mallenby
Wallice Institute of Psychometric Assessment, 1998.
Database: WorldCat

"$275,000 of taxpayer's money wasn't enough!": the federal government of Canada conspiracy
by Terry W Mallenby
Wallice Institute of Psychometric Assessment, 1999
Database: WorldCat

"Alberta premier Ralph Klein's legacy to Canadian criminal justice!"
by Terry Wallice Mallenby
Wallice Institute of Psychometric Assessment, 1999
Database: WorldCat

Alberta crown agent RAE Kubik's legacy to Canada : more fabricated statements by government agent(s)
by Terry W Mallenby
Wallice Institute of Psychometric Assessment, 1999.
Database: WorldCat

The story 'too hot' for the investigative program "The Fifth Estate"!!
by Terry W Mallenby
Wallice Institute of Psychometric Assessment, Applied Studies & Investigative Research, 2000.
Database: WorldCat

Cognitive development : the efficacy of the A Plus Child Development's Project "Head Start" Program in such
development : a review of the "Head Start" Program
by Terry W Mallenby
Institute of Applied Studies, 2002.
Database: WorldCat

Military issue: "bandaged heels & grossly over-sized combat boots"
by Terry Mallenby
Wallice Institute of Psychometric Assessment, 2010.
Database: WorldCat

General W.Z. Natynczyk says "boot fitting procedures were not followed by 748 Comm Sqn, Nanaimo"
by Terry W Mallenby
Institute of Psychometric Assessment, 2010.
Database: WorldCat

Canada's police force: lies, fabrication, perjury ... and much worse?
by Terry Mallenby
Publisher: Charleston, South Carolina : CreateSpace, 2012
Database: WorldCat

## EDUCATIONAL BACKGROUND OF TERRY W. MALLENBY:

OFFICE DE LA LANGUE FRANCAISE:
GOUVERNEMENT DU QUEBEC, OFFICE DE LA LANGUE FRANCAISE ATTESTATION CERTIFICATE #41-0063, DATED 24 MARS, 1986. CONFORMEMENT A L'ARTICLE 35 DE LA CHARTE DE LA LANGUE FRANCAISE, NOUS ATTESTONS QUE TERRY MALLENBY POSSEDE DE LA LANGUE OFFICIELLE DU QUEBEC UNE CONNAISSANCE APPROPRIEE A L'EXERCISE DE SA PROFESSION.

MINISTERE DE L'EDUCATION:
GOUVERNEMENT DU QUEBEC, MINISTERE DE L'EDUCATION RELEVE DES ACQUIS, DATED JUILLET, 1990
FRENCH SECOND LANGUAGE: LEVEL 1, 2 & 3.

DIPLOMA GENERAL SOCIAL WORK, DIPLOMA DATED 8 OCTOBER, 1974
DIPLOMA APPLIED PSYCHOLOGY, DIPLOMA DATED 13 MAY, 1975
CANADIAN INSTITUTE OF SCIENCE & TECHNOLOGY [NOW CALLED "GRANTON INSTITUTE OF TECHNOLOGY"]. COURSES: PEOPLE IN GROUPS; CONFLICT & CHANGE; SOCIOLOGY AS A SCIENCE & SOCIAL WORK HISTORY; SOCIAL INSTITUTIONS, SOCIAL CONTROL & PROBLEMS OF COMMUNICATION; CONCEPTS, METHODS & MODELS; SOCIAL PROCESSES & SOCIAL PROBLEMS; ADAPTATION & HUMAN RELATIONS; PRACTICAL & APPLIED PSYCHOLOGY; GENERAL INDUSTRIAL PSYCHOLOGY; TRAINING FOR MANAGEMENT & MENTAL EFFICIENCY; VOCATIONAL TESTING & INTERVIEWING; INTER-GROUP RELATIONS; THE REVERSE EFFECT.

CERTIFICATE JAIL ADMINISTRATION, CERTIFICATE DATED: 09 FEB, 1976
CERTIFICATE JAIL OPERATIONS, CERTIFICATE DATED: 01 MARCH, 1976
U.S. DEPARTMENT OF JUSTICE, NATIONAL INSTITUTE OF CORRECTIONS, BUREAU OF PRISONS. COURSES: ADMINISTRATION OF OPERATIONS; PERSONNEL & FISCAL MANAGEMENT; COMMUNITY RELATIONS & JAIL PLANNING; CORRECTIONAL HISTORY & JAIL CLIMATE; SUPERVISION, DISCIPLINE & SPECIAL PRISONERS.

CERTIFICATE DRUGS & YOUTH COUNSELING, CERTIFICATE MARCH, 1975
CERTIFICATE ADVANCED CORRECTIONAL COUNSELING, CERT. SEPT., 1975
DOUGLAS COLLEGE. [REFERENCE LETTER BY: R.E. WATKINS, CLASSIFICATION SERVICES COORDINATOR, DATED 1 OCTOBER, 1975]. COURSES: ADVANCED INTERVIEWING & COUNSELING; MARRIAGE & FAMILY COUNSELING; PROBLEMS OF VIOLENCE; PAROLE PREDICTION & SUPERVISION; MEASUREMENT & EVALUATION OF RESEARCH TECHNIQUES; BUREAUCRACIES & CONFLICT; COMMUNITY LIAISON SERVICES; COMPULSORY INTERVIEWING, INMATE CODE & RESTRICTIONS; PAROLE VIOLATION & FORFEITURE; RADICAL THERAPIES & POLYGRAPH.

BACHELOR OF ARTS PSYCHOLOGY
SIMON FRASER UNIVERSITY, DEGREE DATED: MAY, 1970. [REGIONALLY ACCREDITED UNIVERSITY] [COMPLETED IN CANADA][EVALUATED TO U.S.A. EQUIVALENCY BY EDUCATIONAL RECORDS EVALUATION SERVICE, SACRAMENTO, CALIFORNIA][LETTER DATED 10 JANUARY, 1996, REFERENCE #95-01008]
[SIMON FRASER UNIVERSITY RANKING #1, FOR CANADIAN MEDIUM SIZED UNIVERSITIES, MACLEAN'S RANKINGS][LETTER OF REFERENCE BY: DR. H. WEINBERG, ASSOCIATE PROFESSOR, DATED 24 FEBRUARY, 1970][LETTER OF REFERENCE BY: DR. ELINOR AMES, ASSOCIATE PROFESSOR, DATED 17 MARCH, 1971]. COURSES (MATHEMATICS, ENGLISH, OTHER): MATH 101 STATISTICS; MATH 114 FUNDAMENTAL MATH II; ENGL 201 THE STUDY OF LITERATURE; PHIL 100 THEORY OF KNOWLEDGE; EDUC 201 THEORY OF EDUCATION; CC&A 200 THEORY AND PROCESS OF COMMUNICATION; PSA 274 TRADITIONAL ECONOMICS & TECHNOLOGY; PSA 172 ANTHROPOLOGICAL CONCEPTS; BSF 425 LEARNING AND THE PROCESS OF EDUCATION. COURSES (GENERAL & ADVANCED PSYCHOLOGY): PSYC 150 FACTORS OF PERFORMANCE; PSYC 201 EXPERIMENTAL PSYCHOLOGY; PSYC 210 DATA ANALYSIS IN PSYCHOLOGY; PSYC 220 LEARNING; PSYC 230 PERCEPTION; PSYC 240 MOTIVATION; PSYC 320 COGNITIVE PROCESSES; PSYC 325

MEMORY; PSYC 330 SITUATION PERCEPTION; PSYC 340 PSYCHOPATHOLOGY; PSYC 350 DEVELOPMENTAL PSYCHOLOGY; PSYC 360 SOCIAL PSYCHOLOGY; PSYC 370 THEORIES OF PERSONALITY; PSYC 380 PHYSIOLOGICAL PSYCHOLOGY; PSYC 401 HISTORY & SYSTEMS; PSYC 450 DEVELOPMENTAL PSYCHOLOGY SEMINAR; PSYC 480 PHYSIOLOGICAL PSYCHOLOGY SEMINAR. PSYC 310 THEORY OF MEASUREMENT [TESTING EXPERIENCE: WECHSLER INTELLIGENCE SCALE FOR CHILDREN (W.I.S.C.); WECHSLER ADULT INTELLIGENCE SCALE (W.A.I.S.)]; PSYC 496 DIRECTED STUDIES ["EPIDEMIOLOGY OF MENTAL ILLNESS"; NOTE: THE PROJECT FOR DIRECTED STUDIES CONSISTED OF A PATIENT FILE REVIEW OF A PSYCHIATRIC HOSPITAL RELATED TO DETERMINING THE EPIDEMIOLOGY OF MENTAL ILLNESS COMPLETED IN CONJUNCTION WITH FELLOW
STUDENT MS. MARY STEINHAUSER WHO WAS LATER SHOT TO DEATH DURING A HOSTAGE INCIDENT AT THE B.C. PENITENTIARY WHERE WE BOTH WORKED].

BACHELOR OF SOCIAL WORK
MCGILL UNIVERSITY, DEGREE DATED: 8 NOVEMBER, 1988. [REGIONALLY ACCREDITED UNIVERSITY][COMPLETED IN CANADA][EVALUATED TO U.S.A. EQUIVALENCY BY EDUCATIONAL RECORDS EVALUATION SERVICE, SACRAMENTO, CALIFORNIA][LETTER DATED 10 JANUARY, 1996, REFERENCE #95-01008][MCGILL UNIVERSITY RANKING #1, LARGE SIZED UNIVERSITIES IN CANADA, MACLEAN'S RANKINGS][REFERENCE LETTER BY: DR. IRV BINIK, ASSOCIATE PROFESSOR, DATED 6 JUNE, 1986]
[REFERENCE LETTER BY: MRS. LYNN THOMPSON, DATED 27 NOV., 1987][REFERENCE LETTER BY: PETER LEONARD, DIRECTOR, DATED 30 MAY, 1988]. COURSES IN SOCIAL WORK: SW 350 SOCIAL WORK SKILLS LABORATORY; SW 352 PUBLIC SOCIAL SERVICES IN CANADA; SW 353 SOCIAL WORK PRACTICE; SW 354 SOCIAL SERVICES IN HEALTH FIELD; SW 355 FIELD PRACTICE I [SENIOR CITIZENS]; SW 356 FIELD PRACTICE II [SENIOR CITIZENS]; SW 364 INDUSTRIAL SOCIAL WORK; SW 458 SOCIAL POLICY & ADMINISTRATION; SW 420 ADVANCED FIELD PRACTICE I [CHILD PROTECTION]; SW 421 ADVANCED FIELD PRACTICE II [CHILD PROTECTION]; SW 459 ADULT-CHILD SEXUAL RELATIONS: LEGAL ISSUES; SW 475 COMMUNITY ORGANIZATIONS; SW 492 SEMINAR ON FAMILY VIOLENCE; SW 484 SEMINAR ON COMMUNITY ORGANIZATIONS; SW 530 SEMINAR ON SOCIAL PERSPECTIVES OF AGING;
[VOLUNTARY PLACEMENT PRIOR TO PROGRAM AT DOUGLAS PSYCHIATRIC HOSPITAL A MCGILL UNIVERSITY TEACHING HOSPITAL, CONFIRMATION LETTER BY D. DELANEY, DATED 21 NOVEMBER, 1986].

POST-GRADUATE DIPLOMA HEALTH & SOCIAL SERVICES MANAGEMENT,
MCGILL UNIVERSITY [DIPLOMA DATED: 7 JUNE, 1988; REGIONALLY ACCREDITED UNIVERSITY][MCGILL UNIVERSITY RANKING #1, LARGE SIZED UNIVERSITIES IN CANADA, MACLEAN'S RANKINGS][LETTER OF REFERENCE BY: DR. H. COOPERSMITH M.D., ASSISTANT PROFESSOR, DATED 11 NOV., 1987][LETTER OF REFERENCE BY: MR. ROBERT VYNCKE, VILLE MARIE SOCIAL SERVICES, YOUTH PROTECTION, 11 DEC., 1987][LETTER OF REFERENCE BY: MR. ROBIN ELEY, MBA, CA, DIRECTOR, DATED 24 MAY, 1988]
COURSES: 627-101 COLLEGE ALGEBRA & FUNCTIONS; 279-294 LABOR MANAGEMENT RELATIONS; 619-353 HEALTH CARE ORGANIZATION, RISK MANAGEMENT & LIABILITY; 280-331 MANAGEMENT INFORMATION SYSTEMS; 280-211 FINANCIAL ACCOUNTING; 280-222 ORGANIZATIONAL BEHAVIOR; 619-354 HOSPITAL ORGANIZATION & MANAGEMENT; 619-401 EVALUATION OF HEALTH & SOCIAL SERVICE ORGANIZATIONS; 619-452 LEGAL ASPECTS OF HEALTH CARE; 272-423 PERSONNEL ADMINISTRATION; 619-352 DEPARTMENTAL MANAGEMENT IN HEALTH & SOCIAL SERVICES; 629-201 MACRO ECONOMICS; 629-202 MICRO ECONOMICS.

FIRST YEAR AMERICAN LAW COMPLETED
KENSINGTON UNIVERSITY COLLEGE OF LAW [unaccredited school]. [G.P.A. 3.0][COMPLETED IN U.S.A.][STATE APPROVED UNIV.]
[REGISTERED LAW STUDENT, STATE BAR OF CALIFORNIA, REG.#261753028]. COURSES COMPLETED: LL 500 LEGAL WRITING; LL 516 CRIMINAL LAW; LL 512 CONTRACTS; LL 514 TORTS; LL 529 SALES. FIRST YEAR BAR EXAM 24 JUNE, 1997 [CONFIRMATION LETTER 8 AUGUST, 1997].

MASTER OF ARTS [BEHAVIORAL SCIENCES DEPARTMENT]
SIMON FRASER UNIVERSITY, DEGREE DATED: MAY, 1975 [REGIONALLY ACCREDITED UNIVERSITY][G.P.A. 4.0][COMPLETED IN CANADA][EVALUATED TO U.S.A. EQUIVALENCY BY EDUCATIONAL RECORDS EVALUATION SERVICE, SACRAMENTO, CALIFORNIA][LETTER DATED 10 JANUARY, 1996, REFERENCE #95-01008][SIMON FRASER UNIVERSITY RANKING #1, FOR CANADIAN MEDIUM SIZED UNIVERSITIES, MACLEAN'S RANKINGS][LETTER OF RESEARCH BY: A.G. MOODIE, RESEARCH STUDIES & TESTING, BOARD OF SCHOOL TRUSTEES, DATED 16 APRIL, 1974][CONFIRMATION LETTER BY: A.G. MOODIE, RESEARCH STUDIES & TESTING, BOARD OF SCHOOL TRUSTEES, DATED 28 FEB., 1989]. BEHAVIORAL SCIENCES COURSES: CMNS 0800 CONTEMPORARY APPROACHES; CMNS 0801 METHODOLOGY & DESIGN; CMNS 0810 HUMAN FACTORS; CMNS 0820 INTERPERSONAL & GROUP PROCESSES; CMNS 0870 FIELD STUDY & CMNS 898 M.A. THESIS.

PUBLISHED MASTER'S THESIS ENTITLED: "THE MISSING PERSON IN MEASUREMENT TECHNIQUES OF INTERPERSONAL DISTANCE".

COPY APPEARS IN: NATIONAL LIBRARY OF CANADA, OTTAWA, CANADA. THESIS ON MICROFICHE: CALL #BF 469 M35 - AS044138; SUBJECTS - SPACE, INTERPERSONAL RELATIONS].

MASTER OF ARTS & PH.D. PSYCHOLOGY COURSES
AS INDEPENDENT STUDENT UNIVERSITY OF NEW BRUNSWICK [REGIONALLY ACCREDITED UNIVERSITY] & UNIVERSITY OF MANITOBA [REGIONALLY ACCREDITED UNIVERSITY][RESEARCH LETTER BY: DR. G.H. LOWTHER MB, CHB, MEDICAL SUPERINTENDENT, THE MANITOBA SCHOOL, 4 DECEMBER, 1972] [RESEARCH LETTER BY: MR. G.B. LITTLE, VICTORIA SCHOOL, DATED 5 APRIL, 1972][RESEARCH LETTER BY: DR. S.D. SINGH, MEERUT UNIVERSITY, DATED 1 NOVEMBER, 1977 & 17 JANUARY, 1978]
PSYCHOLOGY COURSES: PSYC 6031 ADVANCED STATISTICS; PSYC 6061 SOCIAL PSYCHOLOGY; PSYC 6051 PHYSIOLOGICAL PSYCHOLOGY; PSYC 0738 ADVANCED RESEARCH DESIGN; PSYC 0747 ADVANCED DEVELOPMENTAL PSYCHOLOGY; PSYC 0770 PROBLEMS IN PSYCHOLOGICAL RESEARCH I; PSYC 0772 PROBLEMS IN PSYCHOLOGICAL RESEARCH II; PSYC 0745 GROUP BEHAVIOUR; PSYC 0750 ADVANCED EXPERIMENTAL PSYCHOLOGY; PSYC 0810 SEMINAR ON DEVELOPMENTAL PSYCHOLOGY. TESTING EXPERIENCE: TEST OF NON-VERBAL INTELLIGENCE (T.O.N.I.); MINNESOTA MULTIPHASIC PERSONALITY INVENTORY (M.M.P.I.); SLOSSEN INTELLIGENCE TEST (S.I.T.); CALIFORNIA PSYCHOLOGICAL INVENTORY (C.P.I.); CAREER OCCUPATIONAL PREFERENCE SYSTEM (C.O.P.S.); SIXTEEN PERSONALITY FACTOR QUESTIONNAIRE (16 P.F.).

PH.D. COUNSELING PSYCHOLOGY
KENSINGTON UNIVERSITY [unaccredited school], DEGREE DATED: 26 AUGUST, 1994. [G.P.A. 3.83][COMPLETED IN U.S.A.][STATE APPROVED UNIVERSITY][REFERENCE LETTER BY: DR. WILLIAM KRAUS, DEAN OF FACULTY, DATED 24 AUGUST, 1994][REFERENCE LETTER BY: DR. JAMES LAMBERT, VICE PRESIDENT FOR ACADEMIC AFFAIRS, DATED 12 DEC., 1994].

HUMAN RESOURCES MANAGEMENT PROGRAM COURSES: KU 607 ORGANIZATION BEHAVIOR & MANAGEMENT; KU 516 PERSONNEL MANAGEMENT; KU698 DISSERTATION PROPOSAL.

COUNSELING PSYCHOLOGY COURSES: PSYC 573 PSYCHOPATHOLOGY; PSYC 522 PERSPECTIVES IN ETHOLOGY; PSYC 517 EDUCATIONAL PSYCHOLOGY; PSYC 587 SOCIAL PSYCHOLOGY; PSYC 556 DEPRESSION THEORY; PSYC 574 CHILD PSYCHOPATHOLOGY; PSYC 699 DISSERTATION.

TESTING EXPERIENCE: ADJECTIVE CHECK LIST (A.C.L.); CAREER ABILITY PLACEMENT SURVEY (C.A.P.S.); MASLACH BURNOUT INVENTORY (HUMAN SERVICES SURVEY); CHILD ANXIETY SCALE (C.A.S.); SLOSSON ORAL READING TEST (S.O.R.T.); CLINICAL ANALYSIS QUESTIONNAIRE (C.A.Q.); CANADIAN OCCUPATIONAL INTEREST INVENTORY (C.O.I.I.); MILLION CLINICAL MULTIAXIAL INVENTORY (M.C.M.I.); I.P.A.T. ANXIETY SCALE.

PUBLISHED DOCTORAL DISSERTATION ENTITLED: "INCIDENTS OF PHYSICAL ASSAULT AGAINST CHILD ABUSE INVESTIGATION WORKERS: THE NATURE OF CHILD-ABUSE PROTECTION LEGISLATION AS A POSSIBLE REASON FOR SUCH INCIDENTS: SOME CANADIAN AND AMERICAN EXAMPLES OF INTERNAL POLICIES ATTEMPTING TO DEAL WITH SUCH INCIDENTS: PLACING THE TREND OF SUCH INCIDENTS INTO A THEORETICAL PERSPECTIVE".

PUBLISHED BY: UNIVERSITY MICROFILMS INTERNATIONAL-DISSERTATION SERVICES (THE ONLY CENTRAL SOURCE FOR ACCESSING ALMOST EVERY DOCTORAL DISSERTATION ACCEPTED IN NORTH AMERICA SINCE 1861) RESEARCH ABSTRACTS INTERNATIONAL, VOL. 20(03R), P.1012, ANN ARBOR, MICHIGAN, 1994.

COPY APPEARS IN: HUMANITIES & SOCIAL SERVICES DIVISION, LIBRARY OF CONGRESS, WASHINGTON, D.C. LEGAL DEPOSIT & COPYRIGHT #TX4-167-531.

COPY ALSO APPEARS IN: THE BODLEIAN LAW LIBRARY, OXFORD UNIVERSITY, OXFORD, ENGLAND, CALL # DISS. CRIM. 1994M252.

## PROFESSIONAL EXPERIENCE OF TERRY W. MALLENBY:

NATIONAL DEFENSE RESEARCH, WESTWIN AIR FORCE BASE
["SECRET LEVEL" FEDERAL GOVERNMENT SECURITY CLEARANCE RECEIVED., MILITARY POLICE IDENTIFICATION; PASS # T 38793, DATED 15 MAY, 1972]. UNDER A SUMMER TERM CONTRACT, GATHERED INFORMATION AND COMPLETED DETAILED REPORT FOR THE RESEARCH DIRECTOR, DR. G.H.S. JONES, TRAINING COMMAND HEADQUARTERS ON "THE RELATIVE EFFECTIVENESS OF WHOLE- AND PART-TASK SIMULATORS", DATED 04 AUG., 1972.

CITY COLLEGE LECTURER, VANCOUVER CITY COLLEGE
[LETTER DATED 24 MARCH, 1974]. LECTURED IN ADULT INTEREST EVENING COURSE ENTITLED: "VERBAL AND NON-VERBAL COMMUNICATION AT HOME AND AT WORK".

FEDERAL MANPOWER & EMPLOYMENT COUNSELING
[CONFIRMATION LETTER DATED 24 MARCH, 1971][CONFIRMATION LETTER DATED 29 OCT., 1973]["SECRET LEVEL" SECURITY CLEARANCE RECEIVED][CONFIRMATION MEMO DATED 05 APRIL, 1971] [CONFIRMATION MEMO DATED 06 DEC., 1973][REFERENCE LETTER BY: MRS. LOIS CLARKE, CANADA MANPOWER & IMMIGRATION, DATED 10 JUNE, 1975].

SPECIAL CLIENTS: DISADVANTAGED CLIENTS (DRUG, ALCOHOL, SUBSTANCE ABUSE EMPLOYEES; PHYSICALLY AND MENTALLY HANDICAPPED WORKERS); ARRANGING AND IMPLEMENTING ON-THE-JOB WORK CONTRACTS, INCLUDING SIGNING AUTHORITY ON BEHALF OF THE DEPARTMENT FOR THE IMPLEMENTATION AND PAYMENT OF SUCH CONTRACTS. ALSO: NORMAL DUTIES OF A MANPOWER (EMPLOYMENT) COUNSELOR.

MEDIA ANNOUNCEMENTS: ANNOUNCED "JOB SHORTAGES" ON LOCAL T.V. & RADIO PROGRAM WHILE AT DAWSON CREEK DISTRICT OFFICE.

TRAINING SESSIONS: CONDUCTED CREATIVE JOB SEARCH TECHNIQUES TRAINING AND PRESENTATION  [CONFIRMATION MEMO DATED 20 - 22 MARCH, 1974].

AGENCY PRESENTATIONS: PRESENTED TO ALLIED ASSOCIATIONS THE TYPE OF SERVICES OFFERED BY THE DEPARTMENT [CONFIRMATION LETTER BY MS. A.M. HILL DATED 15 MAY, 1974][CONFIRMATION LETTER BY S.L. WOLCH DATED 18 APRIL, 1974][CONFIRMATION LETTER BY S.L. WOLCH DATED 29 MAY, 1974].

COURSES COMPLETED: INDUSTRIAL TRAINING-SKILL SHORTAGES; TRAINING IN INDUSTRY; OUTREACH AND LEAP PROJECTS; SPECIAL DIAGNOSTIC SERVICES; IMMIGRATION SERVICES; ADULT BASIC EDUCATION PROGRAMS; MANPOWER MOBILITY PROGRAMS; LABOR MARKET INFORMATION AND TRENDS; INTERVIEWING TECHNIQUES; COUNSELING 101 AND 102 [CONFIRMATION MEMO DATED 26 - 30 APRIL, 1971]; CLASSIFICATION AND DIRECTORY OF OCCUPATIONAL CODES.

SUPREME COURT EXPERIENCE & TESTING EXPERIENCE: CONDUCTED G.A.T.B. (GENERAL APTITUDE TEST BATTERY) TESTING; WAS "EXPERT WITNESS" IN SUPREME COURT OF B.C. CASE GIVING TESTIMONY ON G.A.T.B. TESTING COMPLETED, RE-TRAINING PROGRAMS AVAILABLE FOR ACCIDENT VICTIM WORKER, WITH MARKET/LABOR TRENDS AND PROJECTED SALARY [CONFIRMATION LETTER BY HOROWITZ & TICK, DATED 11 APRIL, 1974][CONFIRMATION LETTER BY ORECK, CHERNOFF & TICK, DATED 28 FEB., 1989] .

STATE PROBATION SUPERVISION & PRE-DISPOSITION REPORTS*
[CERTIFICATE OF CONDUCT, ROYAL NEWFOUNDLAND CONSTABULARY, CERTIFICATE DATED 04 FEB., 1994]. SUPERVISION OF PROBATION, COMMUNITY SERVICE &  COUNSELING OF YOUNG OFFENDERS.
YOUTH COURT EXPERIENCE:  PRE-DISPOSITION REPORT PRESENTATIONS AT YOUTH COURT.

*Newfoundland - The Lieutenant-Governor in Council may designate probation officers appointed under the Department of Social Services Act to act as probation officers for the purposes of this Act and may designate probation officers appointed under this Act to carry out the duties of probation officers for the purposes of the Department of Social Services Act.*

STATE CHILD PROTECTION & CHILD WELFARE SOCIAL WORKER
[CONFIRMATION LETTER 10 AUG., 1990][CONFIRMATION ASSESSMENT TO PERMANENT STATUS DATED 11 MARCH, 1991][REFERENCE LETTER BY: MS. KATHERINA LANZ, DATED 22 JUNE, 1990][REFERENCE LETTER BY: MR. DAVID R. BUSSIERE, DATED 9 JULY, 1990]. INTAKE, INVESTIGATION AND ASSESSMENT OF CHILD WELFARE/CHILD PROTECTION COMPLAINTS; JOINT INTERVIEWS WITH R.C.M.P. RELATED TO CHILD SEXUAL/PHYSICAL ABUSE OR ASSAULT. FAMILY COURT EXPERIENCE: PRESENTATION AT FAMILY COURT; COUNSELING FOR CHILDREN SUBJECTED TO ABUSE, AS WELL AS COUNSELING FOR PARENT(S) AND FAMILIES. DAY CARE INVESTIGATION & ASSESSMENT [CONFIRMATION LETTER 31 MARCH, 1992]. FOSTER HOME SUPERVISION & ASSESSMENT; INFANTS FOR ADOPTION; CHANGE OF NAME ACT. COURSES COMPLETED: STPS #6000 UNDERSTANDING WIFE BATTERING COURSE [CONFIRMATION LETTER DATED 8 JANUARY, 1992].

FEDERAL CLASSIFICATION OFFICER MAXIMUM PRISON & PRE-PAROLE
[CONFIRMATION LETTER DATED 16 SEPTEMBER, 1974][SOLICITOR GENERAL IDENTIFICATION PASS # 10631, DATED 04 SEPT., 1975]["SECRET LEVEL" CLEARANCE REQUIRED AND RECEIVED, CONFIRMATION MEMO DATED 06 DEC., 1973][SECURITY CLEARANCE CONFIRMATION LETTER, DATED 10 SEPT., 1990][SECURITY CLEARANCE CONFIRMATION LETTER, DATED 16 NOV., 1990][REFERENCE LETTER BY: MS. MARY STEINHAUSER MSW, CLASSIFICATION OFFICER, DATED 2 APRIL, 1975][REFERENCE LETTER BY: W. MORT, DIRECTOR, DATED 24 JULY, 1975][REFERENCE LETTER BY: W. ROMPF, SENIOR STAFFING OFFICER, DATED 7 AUGUST, 1975][REFERENCE LETTER BY: R.E. WATKINS, CLASSIFICATION SERVICES COORDINATOR, DATED 1 OCTOBER, 1975].

CASE MANAGEMENT: CLASSIFICATION OFFICER AT FEDERAL MAXIMUM SECURITY PENITENTIARY RESPONSIBILITY FOR MAXIMUM SECURITY INMATES (B.C. PENITENTIARY) AS WELL AS EXPERIENCE WITH MEDIUM /MINIMUM/PROTECTIVE CUSTODY INMATES (MOUNTAIN PRISON), WITH REPRESENTATION AND MEMBERSHIP PARTICIPATION ON INSTITUTIONAL WORK PLACEMENT BOARD, INTER- AND INTRA-REGIONAL TRANSFER BOARDS, PSYCHIATRIC AND CASE CONFERENCE BOARD, CLASSIFICATION BOARD.

PAROLE BOARD EXPERIENCE: INSTITUTIONAL REPRESENTATIVE AT THE NATIONAL PAROLE BOARD HEARINGS REGARDING PRE-PAROLE REPORTS.

CRIMINAL COURT EXPERIENCE: PRESENTATION AT CRIMINAL COURT. SUCCESSFUL CANDIDATE BILINGUAL CLASSIFICATION OFFICER [COMPETITION #75-CPS-PAC-IV-14; CONFIRMATION LETTER DATED 30 JANUARY, 1976].

HIGH RISK BONUS: RECEIVED PENNOLOGICAL FACTOR FOR FREQUENT CONTACT WITH MAXIMUM AND MEDIUM SECURITY FEDERAL INMATES (INCARCERATED FOR MORE THAN TWO YEARS)[CONFIRMATION MEMO DATED 20 JUNE, 1975].

COURSES COMPLETED: CANADIAN PENITENTIARY STAFF TRAINING SESSIONS AT STAFF TRAINING COLLEGE IN EDMONTON, ALBERTA 1974; DRUGS & YOUTH COUNSELING, DOUGLAS COLLEGE, 1975 [REFERENCE LETTER: R.E. WATKINS, CLASSIFICATION SERVICES COORDINATOR, DATED 1 OCTOBER, 1975]; HUMAN SOCIAL FUNCTIONING WORKSHOP TRAINING, 1975 [REFERENCE LETTER DATED 15 JANUARY, 1975].

STATE YOUNG OFFENDER RESIDENT UNIT SUPERVISOR
[CONFIRMATION LETTER DATED 08 OCTOBER, 1992]. MANAGES ALL ASPECTS OF THE OPERATION
OF A COTTAGE-BASED LIVING UNIT IN A LARGE SECURE CUSTODY AND REMAND FACILITY FOR
YOUNG OFFENDERS.

ACTING DISTRICT MANAGER IN STATE SOCIAL SERVICES DEPARTMENT
[CONFIRMATION E MAILS DATED 12 DEC., 1991; 09 DEC., 1991; 13 SEPT., 1991; 16 SEPT., 1991; 04 - 05
SEPT., 1991 & 21 - 22 - 23 JAN., 1992]. RESPONSIBLE FOR THE MANAGEMENT FRONT LINE SOCIAL
WORK STAFF (CHILD WELFARE, CHILD PROTECTION, YOUTH CORRECTIONS, SOCIAL
ASSISTANCE, SERVICES TO THE ELDERLY, REHABILITATIVE SERVICES, ADOPTION & POST
ADOPTION, SERVICES TO THE MENTALLY & PHYSICALLY CHALLENGED, INDEPENDENCE
PROGRAMS, ETC), FINANCIAL ASSISTANCE OFFICERS, CHILD MANAGEMENT SPECIALIST,
COMMUNITY DEVELOPMENT WORKERS, CLERICAL AND SUPPORT STAFF IN A DISTRICT SOCIAL
SERVICES OFFICE IN RURAL NEWFOUNDLAND, WITH A TERRITORY OF SOME 1500 SQUARE MILES.
THOROUGH KNOWLEDGE OF THE CHILD WELFARE ACT, THE SOCIAL ASSISTANCE ACT, THE
ADOPTION OF CHILDREN'S ACT, THE YOUNG OFFENDER'S ACT, ETC.,
INCLUDING ALL PROVINCIAL LEGISLATION, POLICY AND PROCEDURES RELATED TO ALL OF THE
ABOVE NOTED PROGRAMS. KNOWLEDGE OF COLLECTIVE AGREEMENT.

OPERATIONS MANAGER SECURE CUSTODY YOUNG OFFENDER INSTITUTION
[CONFIRMATION LETTER BY G. SKINNER DATED 16 MARCH, 1994][CONFIRMATION ASSESSMENT
TO PERMANENT STATUS DATED 16 MARCH, 1994]. ADMINISTERS, DIRECTS AND MANAGES THE
OVERALL FRONT LINE OPERATIONAL AND PROGRAM FUNCTIONS OF A LARGE PROVINCIAL
SECURE CUSTODY AND REMAND FACILITY (WITH A COMPLEMENT OF 220 STAFF) FOR YOUNG
OFFENDERS; ENSURES THE MAINTENANCE OF PROPER PERSONNEL FUNCTIONS IN ACCORDANCE
WITH POLICY AND PROCEDURES.

MANAGEMENT COURSES COMPLETED: EDP #3007 PREPARATION OF EVIDENCE [CONFIRMATION
MEMO DATED 20 SEPT., 1993]; EFFECTIVE SUPERVISION [CONFIRMATION MEMO DATED 19 OCT.,
1993 &  DATED 23 NOV., 1993]; LABOR RELATIONS & THE LINE MANAGER [CONFIRMATION MEMO
DATED 04 NOV., 1993]; LEADERSHIP & MOTIVATION [CONFIRMATION MEMO DATED 06 JAN., 1994];
EFFECTIVE MANAGEMENT [CONFIRMATION MEMO DATED 10 JAN., 1994]; MANAGING CONFLICT
[CONFIRMATION MEMO DATED 11 JAN., 1994]; PROBLEM SOLVING [CONFIRMATION MEMO DATED
18 JAN., 1994]; CONDUCTING EFFECTIVE MEETINGS [CONFIRMATION MEMO DATED 10 JAN., 1994].

FIRST AID & EMERGENCY SCENE MANAGEMENT COURSES: FIRST AID TRAINING [CONFIRMATION
MEMO DATED 10 MAY, 1994]; EMERGENCY SCENE MANAGEMENT -ARTIFICIAL RESPIRATION;
CHOKING -WOUNDS & BLEEDING; SHOCK, UNCONSCIOUSNESS & FAINTING; JOINT INJURIES,
STRAINS & RESCUE CARRIES; MULTIPLE INJURY MOVEMENT -HEART ATTACK & STROKE; ONE-
RESCUER CPR [CERTIFICATE TO HEART SAVER LEVEL]; MEDICAL CONDITIONS [DIABETES,
EPILEPSY, CONVULSIONS & ALLERGIES; ST. JOHN'S AMBULANCE CERTIFICATE: SAFETY
ORIENTED FIRST AID: STANDARD LEVEL: ELECTIVE MODULES - 06, 08, 12, 13, 18, 19, 20, 21.

OTHER COURSES COMPLETED: INTRODUCTION TO COMPUTER BASICS: PARTS I & II;
UNDERSTANDING DOS -WINDOWS 3.1; FILE MANAGER -UNDERSTANDING NETWORKS;
WORDPERFECT 5.2 -MS MAIL -MS SCHEDULE; [CONFIRMATION LETTER DATED 29 DECEMBER,
1993][CONFIRMATION CERTIFICATE DATED FALL, 1993/WINTER, 1994].

COURT EXPERIENCE: SUBPOENA TO WITNESS, SUPREME COURT, DATED 1993; SUBPOENA TO
WITNESS, STATE COURT, 1993.

www.ingramcontent.com/pod-product-compliance
Lightning Source LLC
Chambersburg PA
CBHW081836170526
45167CB00007B/2830

* 9 7 8 1 5 0 2 9 1 0 8 5 1 *